Back to the Drawing Board!

Wolf Von Eckardt

Illustrated by Forrest Wilson

Back to the Drawing Board!
Planning Livable Cities

New Republic Books, Washington, D.C.

For Judith

Published in 1978 by
New Republic Books
1220 19th St., N.W.
Washington, D.C. 20036

New Republic Books would like to thank the following
copyright holder for permission to use the line from the song
"Big Yellow Taxi," by Joni Mitchell. Copyright © 1969,
Siquomb Pub. Co., used by permission.

Library of Congress Cataloging in Publication Data
Von Eckardt, Wolf.
    Back to the drawing board!
    Bibliography: p.
    Includes index.
    1. City planning.   2. City planning—United States.
3. Architecture—Human factors.   I. Title.
HT166.V66   309.2'62   78-12257
ISBN 0-915220-45-8

Trade distribution by Simon and Schuster
A Division of Gulf & Western Corporation
New York, New York 10020
Ordering No. 24580

Printed in the United States of America

Contents

II Abstract Architecture

III Search for Community

IV The New Urban Vision

Rehabilitation of slum houses by the well-to-do is a blessing,
provided the displaced poor are helped to new homes close
to new employment opportunities.

Human needs rather than aesthetic abstractions, the dictates
of conservation rather than quick profits, must inform a new
architecture.

I The New Mood

1   The View from My Window

Through the window by my typewriter, I see the city change. A new mood in America is changing it.

In the winter of 1963, when we moved from suburban Parkwood to Hillyer Place, just north of Dupont Circle in downtown Washington, D.C., there were only elderly residents, mostly widows, living in the 21 Victorian townhouses on our one-block street. Directly across from our house was a red brick mansion, the Swiss Legation, built in the 1880s. It was not spectacular, as Victorian mansions go, but had quiet dignity and seemed proud of its remaining duties, which no longer included representing the Swiss Confederation. The legation had moved to the first modern-style building in the American capital in 1938. Now the old mansion provided modest comfort to a dozen or so genteel, elderly roomers who never saw their landlord. It also guarded the entrance to Hillyer Place, protecting the tranquility of our street from the noisy commercialism of Connecticut Avenue.

Most people thought this a lost cause, convinced that our quiet row would soon surrender to the uptown march of glossy office buildings. All the once-charming residential streets south of us, streets where trees had been taller than buildings, had already turned into the unsightly jumble of combustion engines, advertising signs, parking lots, stores, and office buildings. The Presbyterians had abandoned their spirited

Richardson-Romanesque church on the corner of N Street to the wrecking balls, and moved to a ghastly modern kitsch cathedral at the edge of the city. The woman who owned the parking lot next to the Swiss Legation, as well as acres of parking lots all over town, had every right to expect that the old mansion would soon yield to attrition. She bought it in hopes of extending her parking lot and eventually, of profiting on another glossy office building.

Attrition worked fast. First, the city obliged and ordered the mansion vacated because of building code violations. It was boarded in such cursory fashion that hippies found it easy to break in and camp inside, starting fires when they sterilized their needles. The owner made a futile attempt to have the property rezoned from residential to commercial, but never tried to secure it against vandals, drug addicts and pyromaniacs. Then one morning, without warning, she silenced our complaints with the roar of bulldozers. Over the counter she obtained a demolition permit from the same city which, a few years earlier, had declared Hillyer Place a registered landmark worthy of historic preservation for its "contribution to the cultural heritage . . . visual beauty and interest." (Since then, the D.C. City Council grants registered landmark buildings a three-month stay of execution so they can rally their defense.)

Following the murder of Dr. Martin Luther King, Washingtonians watched thick, ugly smoke from the burning ghetto drift toward the White House. For a week we lived under curfew, occupied by the National Guard. Along our main streets, soldiers, armed with loaded tommy guns, were posted every 40 feet or so. This trauma, and the recession, slowed the march of progress the parking lot owner had counted on. Tired of our complaints about weeds, mud, and illegally parked cars, she surprised my neighbors, the Tuckers, one day with a letter that said yes, we could turn the vacant Swiss Legation site into a neighborhood park, at our own expense and risk, of course.

It was no Tuileries. A friend of Anne Tucker's, a young

architect, sketched a rough layout of flower beds made of old rail ties. Norman Tucker brought the rail ties for a case of whiskey at the marshaling yards. Tegi McGregor and Liz Weiner helped the Tuckers collect money. They raised $240 in three or four blocks, using $180 for top soil, $40 for the case of whiskey, and $20 for renting the truck that hauled the rail ties. A nearby plant shop donated some shrubs, and anyone in the neighborhood who felt like it planted seeds or seedlings. We had a block party and grandiously called the improvised effort "Hillyer Park."

As I watched it grow, the new mood became evident.

There was a new concern for the environment, for the whole earth. I saw people pick up bits of trash as they passed by. Even the drunks who were bedding down on the rail ties were careful to roll into the gravel, not the flowers. Someone brought an old telephone cable spool that made a convenient lunch table for lovers from the office buildings nearby.

The second summer of our neighborhood garden, I heard young voices and happy squeals. I counted eleven frolicking children. They all lived nearby. Young people were coming back into the city.

And that changed city life. It also affected the view from my window. Thousands of new little neighborhood parks all over the cities of America were being built. Some, like the one across

the street from me, developed spontaneously. Others were planned and built by authorities, usually in response to an aroused citizenry.

Citizens spoke up against freeways, urban renewal, high-rise intrusions and other unwanted changes around their homes. They demanded a voice in decisions affecting their way of life. As neighbors banded together to plan their protests and actions, to learn about zoning and the complex ins and outs of municipal government, a new sense of neighborhood developed, a new sense of militancy. It rose first in the black ghettos of the troubled sixties, but the techniques and rhetoric of protest and citizen organization soon spread to the wealthier, white districts, and to the suburbs as well. White middle-class people got just as angry as blacks about the deterioration of urban life.

Where I live, another assertion of the emerging urban spirit came when Mrs. Chaconas told Claudia Lane that she was tired of running her Crystal City restaurant, and was about to sell it to Gino's.

My neighborhood is mixed—"pluralistic" is the fashionable term. Southwest of Dupont Circle there are old rowhouses teeming with college students, and a sprinkling of new apartment buildings full of government workers. Crossing through the Circle, like a lode of gold through rock, is the Embassy Row of Massachusetts Avenue, providing us with special police who wear flashy gold trim on their uniforms. Northwest of the Circle is beginning to look like Georgetown. But we still have simple neighborhood shops and restaurants, rather than boutiques and bistros. Across Connecticut Avenue, northeast of the Circle, moderate income black families are increasingly yielding their rowhouses to urban pioneers—black and white professionals who buy houses, renovate them on their own, and call them "townhouses."

All these people, except the poorest, used to eat and meet at Mrs. Chaconas's Crystal City at the corner of R Street and Connecticut Avenue, where Claudia Lane worked as a waitress.

The food was good, and the price was right. Crystal City had a sidewalk cafe, and in summer, people would sit and talk over Greek salad and beer or wine, until all hours of the night. Crystal City was a neighborhood center.

But Mrs. Chaconas was ready to retire, and a grease fire hastened her decision. Gino's took an option and made plans to remodel the restaurant into one of its computerized, fast-food dispensaries. Claudia Lane sounded the alarm and news spread like another grease fire. An "Ad Hoc Committee to Prevent Ginocide" pinned communiques on trees, issued "Ginocide" T-shirts, and got more than 2,000 people to sign a petition. The term "Ginocide" was, of course, a misnomer. Claudia Lane, then 22 years old, did not mean for Gino's to be killed—she just did not want Gino's to kill a neighborhood amenity.

Just about everyone in the area joined the cause—poor blacks, middle-class blacks, small business people, landlords, the elderly women who held on to their elderly homes, students, artists, the liberal Brookings and conservative Institute for Defense Analysis Ph.d.'s who breakfast at Schwartz's drugstore—even some winos who hang out in the little triangular park at Q Street. A neighborhood delegation journeyed to Valley Forge, Pennsylvania, to picket Gino's national headquarters.

Gino's surrendered. Crystal City is now a French restaurant, its sidewalk cafe jammed from May to October, its fare mediocre and expensive. But at least it is not a fast-food chain dispensary. For a price, you can sit and linger and watch the world go by, rather than eat on the run.

Neighborhoods everywhere have found themselves in common resistance to technological "improvements" that turn out to be "deprovements," to use Joseph Alsop's word. Negative protest often leads to positive cooperation. It happened around Dupont Circle.

But there wasn't anything any of us could do when, out of a gray winter sky, the bulldozers appeared again one morning on the lot across the street from my window. They ripped up "Hillyer Park," including the shrubs and bulbs we had lovingly planted, and dug foundations for ye four tiny towne houses.

They are half built as I write, and perfect little horrors: phony colonial-federal-Adams style with mullioned windows, dormers, keystones and fanlights, in a variety of ugly-colored bricks. They are as appropriate an entree to our pastel-colored Victorian street as Gino-burgers are to a lunch of lobster salad and champagne. Architecture, as I shall discuss later in this book, still has a long way to go.

But we have also come a long way. The new little horror townhouses—and they are legion, not only in Washington, but in most cities now—prove that cities are becoming respectable places to live again. People want to make the cities human, rather than high-rising and fast-food efficient.

In its new mood, as I see it through my window, America is beginning to settle down.

2   Settling Down in America

The return to the city—as yet a trickle statistically, but psychologically an important trend—is due not only to disenchantment with the green dream of suburbia or a sudden passion for townhouses. There is, I believe, a deeper, perhaps subconscious feeling that there is no more escape, that the time has come to stay put, to make the best of the America we have. There is no other.

We have been a nation on the run. The white settlers ran from old world tyranny and poverty. The Indians ran from the white man. Blacks ran from slavery. We all kept running.

We all wanted to breathe free and that meant moving on, westward and upward. It did not seem to matter if we made a mess. It would soon be left behind. A mess left behind was progress. We believed that progress was perpetual, affluence kept flowing, and man could be perfected.

This belief, the American Ethos, stems from the Western legacy: Judaism, Christianity, humanism, and now, materialism or economic determinism. It holds, as the ecologist Ian McHarg put it, that since the Bible says man is

created in the image of God, he *is* like God "and therefore given dominion over all creatures and things. He is enjoined to subdue the earth."

It is a reckless belief which, for all our noble and political ideals, caused us to murder Indians and kill buffalo, hold human beings in slavery, and rape the land. We continue to dam rivers and flood valleys, gash hills with strip mines and freeways, devastate waterfronts with malodorous industries, demolish our architectural heritage, litter a continent with the screaming neon of greedy commercialism and, as the song has it, "Pave paradise and put up a parking lot."

The ravage was sanctioned at the start of our nationhood. The Land Ordinance of 1785, passed by the Continental Congress, provided that all land was to be laid out in rectangular townships of six square miles. Each township was to be subdivided into 36 square sections of one square mile, or 640 acres.

Half the land was to be sold by the township; the other half in public auction for a minimum of one dollar per acre, plus the surveying costs. Some sections were set aside for Revolutionary War veterans, some were reserved for the national government, and one for a public school.

For the next century, until the frontier was closed, the grid governed the settlement of the country. The six-mile lines often became highways; the section lines became country roads. The system speeded the westward trek. It made surveying easy. It demonstrated the white man's dominance over nature, disregarding hill or dale, mountain or canyon, brook or stream. In San Francisco, the grid streets run straight up steep hills, causing radiators to boil and brakes to burn.

The checkerboard pattern made uniform lots for easy sales. It made the parcels simple to describe in deeds or from the auction block. It imposed a dreadful monotony and mediocrity on our country.

After the American Revolution most of the land was in the public domain. It belonged to the American people. John Quincy Adams warned against giving it away for unrestricted exploitation. He argued that the land should be used for the public benefit, as well as for private profit.

But Thomas Jefferson, Andrew Jackson, and overwhelming popular demand insisted on unlimited and rapid westward expansion to make ours a nation of individual freeholders. Manifest Destiny was not only our resolve to develop a continent, but also to get rich—quick and easy.

The truth is, we never wanted compact communities; we never wanted to build those gleaming alabaster cities. Jefferson viewed "great cities as pestilential to the morals, the health and the liberties of man," and most Americans agreed. Gerald Ford said much the same about destitute New York City.

But now the continent is conquered. We have run out of "West," we are running out of riches, and we are being forced to recognize that there are limits to economic growth and collective upward mobility. We must change our habits of waste. The affluent society will have to become a conserving society.

All this, I believe, makes America a little more humble, but by no means discouraged, as we smile wanly at contradictions in our national life.

"There once was a nation of two hundred million people," wrote one of America's most lucid urbanists—Wilfred Owen of The Brookings Institution—in what he called a "fable" on urban America. This nation, he continued, "was the most powerful country in all the world. At the national level the inhabitants were very rich. At the local level they often turned out to be quite poor. And as luck would have it, they all lived at the local level."

They had, to hitchhike on Owen's fable, the most dazzling technology in history, leading, as someone put it, "from know-how to nowhere." They wrapped the glasses in every motel room in cellophane, for the sanitary protection of the guests, but the water was polluted. They conditioned their air, though it was poisoned by carbon monoxide. They drove fast cars, but it took them twice as long to get from the edge of town to the center than it had for their grandparents.

They took pity on slum dwellers, but their expensive urban

renewal programs destroyed more low-cost housing than it built. Middle-class women received the best education they had ever enjoyed, but were used mostly as chauffeurs.

They improved education by making it fun and easy for children to learn, but all the children learned was easy fun. Health care became even more expensive, but medical services became worse.

They worked very hard to make and keep politics democratic, and accountants were instructed to call bosses by their first names. When it came time to go home, the bosses went to another part of town. In fact, the executives making more than $100,000 a year went to a suburban subdivision for executives making more than $100,000 a year. The middle-income executives went to the middle-income executive subdivisions. The not-so-fancy white-collar workers went to not-so-fancy white-collar neighborhoods. The blue-collar workers went to ethnic neighborhoods. Middle-income singles went to downtown luxury apartments. The elderly were kept in homes or "leisure worlds" for the elderly. Blacks stayed in the ghetto.

In addition, this rich nation of 200 million people segregated every square inch of its country—light industrial zones and heavy industrial zones, this kind of commercial zone and that kind of commercial zone, and residential zones for all classes of residents. Zoning made it as difficult as possible for a kid with rich parents to meet a kid with poor parents. It made certain that a white-collar worker would not be found in the same bar as a blue-collar worker. Today our habitat has become so thoroughly segregated that society threatens to disintegrate.

Besides being zoned, America's land in metropolitan areas is being wasted. It is being wasted in a pattern of development that, in the words of urban critic Donald Canty, "scatters the focal points of life, defies rational transportation systems, perpetuates social division and injustice—and turns the initial cost of waste into life-cycle costs of huge dimensions. It is a pattern called sprawl."

Urban sprawl is a cataclysmic happening that began with the post-World War II baby boom, affluence, federal home-loan guarantees, and a frenzy of freeway construction. And worse than its insane waste of money, energy, natural resources and land, it has made us unhappy.

Consider the drug scene, the divorce rate, the escape into all manner of cults, pseudoreligions, hedonism, quackery, and psychiatry. No longer truly at home where we live, many Americans believe they must "get in touch with themselves," assisted by psychics or psychoanalysts. Looking out for Number One is the motto and "self-realization" is the goal. The new American frontier seems to be the Ego.

Those who cannot afford snake oil or witchcraft fight their environment with aggressive noise. They turn up their transistor radios, or gun their motorcycles. They turn to vandalism and crime.

The young immerse themselves in deafening and mind-numbing "vibes," generated by 120-decibel rock. Everyone else seems addicted to the continuous din of Muzak or other electronic sound drizzle. These noise addicts no more enjoy the music than chain smokers enjoy tobacco. They veil the reality of their surroundings with the smoke of sound.

Women who felt wasted in suburbia were always told by their psychiatrists to accept their femininity and take Miltown. The answer to middle-class discomfort is to see a shrink, join an encounter group, or do yoga. The answer to rats, clogged toilets, and other distresses of poverty is a visit from a social worker. When escape seems impractical, we are told to adjust.

Even the designers of the human environment would rather change us than change what they have wrought. When the roof on one of his houses was leaking, Frank Lloyd Wright told the hapless owner to get a bucket. When their glass boxes get too hot, modern architects prescribe more air conditioners. When their cities get jammed with automobiles, city planners cut down trees, narrow the sidewalks, build more freeways, and turn more buildings into parking lots to accommodate even more automobiles.

All that is idiotic, of course.

It is time to adjust architecture and urban development to the needs of people, rather than try to adjust people to the ego trips of architects and the profiteering of urban developers. Americans are beginning to understand that this is our land and our home.

This new urban awareness, followed by the new ecological awareness, began in 1962 with the publication of Rachel Carson's *Silent Spring.* Eight years later, largely on the instigation of Senator Gaylord A. Nelson, young Americans celebrated "Earth Day" for the first time. In 1972, the ecology on "Spaceship Earth" became the international concern of governments represented at the United Nations conference on the environment in Stockholm. Four years later in Vancouver, the broad concern for the environment focused on human settlements. The "Habitat" conference of the United Nations was specific and constructive. It dealt primarily with the challenge of decent housing for the rapidly proliferating populations of developing countries. But it also showed the industrialized countries that the degradation of the earth—air, water, and land pollution, the depletion of natural resources, the dwindling of wild life and wilderness—literally starts at home. Where and how we build our homes and communities determines the quality—not only of human life—but of all life on earth.

We are beginning to see that in a democracy it is no more necessary to have delinquent and badly planned communities than it is to have corrupt politicians and badly conceived laws. We can speak up. We can make our needs and interests known. We can participate in planning and building our places to live, and see to it that our habitat endeavors are socially just, physically healthy, aesthetically pleasant, and culturally stimulating; that they serve, to use August Heckscher's phrase, "the public happiness."

We have more to gain, I believe, by consulting our friendly neighborhood planners than our psychiatrists. We can achieve more to improve our relationship with others by participating in community planning, rather than group therapy encounters.

What ails us—most of us, anyway—is not that we are incapable of living a satisfactory and creative life in harmony with ourselves, but that our habitat does not offer sufficient opportunities. It hems us in. It isolates us. It irritates and disrupts.

This is not to say that better community planning and development can create utopian communities that will produce perfect, utopian men, women, and children. Of course not. Good architects have designed good housing projects, but the people who moved in remained the same old bastards they always were. Good architects have designed humane jails that respected the prisoners' dignity, but the rate of recidivism was no less than that of barbaric penitentiaries.

Better environmental planning and building can bring old and young together. It can provide for spontaneous encounters, give teenagers outlets for their energies, and toddlers safe freedom to play. It can give all of us stimulation and recreation.

It can give us time or steal it with endless journeys to work.

Architects and planners, thank heaven, do not write the script (it is an inevitable disaster when they try). But they do provide the stage setting for human drama. The actors should see that the set fits the play.

Constructive participation, to be sure, requires some knowledge and understanding of what we are participating in. We need more public education in the history and fundamentals of architecture and urban design. There is nothing difficult about this, except, perhaps, the gobbledygook that architects and urbanists use to obfuscate their craft. Don't let them fool you. All there is to environmental design—or all there should be—is the application of common sense to common problems.

A growing number of Americans now want to see that common sense applied. They want to settle down, pitch in, and make our habitat more livable and attractive. And that is what the new mood is all about.

It is bolstered by new circumstances. The baby boom of the fifties and early sixties is over. Except for immigration (half of it illegal from south of the border), the United States seems to have come close to zero population growth—that blissful state where the number of babies born equals the number of people who die. Schools built only a few years ago now stand empty, or are converted to other uses.

As important as the baby bust is the fact that the in-migration into the big cities of rural families from the South and Puerto Rico has come to a halt. Between 1970 and 1974, nearly 13 million unemployed farm workers poured into the ghettos of New York City, Chicago, Detroit, Newark, St. Louis, and other old manufacturing cities. Fourteen million white taxpayers moved out. Now, it seems, the blacks stay south, finding jobs in the new industries of the "sun belt."

The churning within our population will continue, however. People move as the economy shifts, and while old industries die, new ones spring up elsewhere. Immigrants arrive in search of jobs and housing. People move as they start families, or when their children set out on their own and their homes become too large.

The drop in the birthrate, demographers tell us, is more than offset by new household formations. This means that more people seek separate places to live—youngsters leaving home earlier than they used to; people wishing to live together, married or unmarried; people who are divorced; and elderly people who wish to maintain their own households.

They seek something different than the detached, single-family suburban homes. They want communal laundries, community rooms, swimming pools, tennis courts, and golf courses. They like to live close to their work, to shops, restaurants, entertainment, and recreation. They would like to live in the center city if they did not have to fear crime and if the city were more inviting. Many of them dream of living in a remodeled Back Bay mansion, a Georgetown house, or a high-ceilinged East Side Manhattan apartment with a marble mantle in the living room.

The phenomenal growth of the historic preservation movement is more than a fashion. Not long ago, saving old buildings—the kind George Washington slept in—was almost the exclusive domain of the proverbial little tennis-shoed ladies. Today, preservation has become as much a cause for the young as for the old, the progressive as well as the conservative. It is part of the new mood, a mood that has become less concerned with the standard of living than the standard of life, a mood that would not have man subdue the earth but recognizes that humans are part of the natural ecology.

It is a mood that puts "progress" in quotation marks, protests fast-food chains, stopped the SST, is wary of the Concorde and nuclear power plants. It is a mood that would rather recycle than waste natural materials and attractive old buildings.

It is a rediscovery of what civilization used to be all about.

3 The City That Was

The meaning of the word "civilization" has changed since the Marquis de Mirabeau coined it in 1757. Cities—being the generators of civilization—reflect that change.

As the Marquis and Europe's eighteenth-century gentry saw it, *la civilisation* stood for the promotion of law and peaceful, well-mannered behavior; the advancement of knowledge and cultivation of the arts; and as Jefferson once said, "the pursuit of happiness." Civilization denoted faith in reason. It meant, as historian John U. Nef said, "The hope, and sometimes the conviction, that man's intelligence was getting the upper hand over his violent propensities."

This hope, and sometimes conviction, governed human intercourse and state craft, as well as the design and building of cities. It was the intellectual premise on which this republic was founded.

In our time, however, a Spengler or Toynbee would not use the word civilization to denote a state of mind, but the state of technology in a given culture. Today, civilization does not mean humane human conduct, but mechnical proficiency; not politesse, but plumbing. We now speak of different civilizations: Mayan, Roman, Chinese, North American, and the rest. In the old sense, in fact, our Western civilization is hardly civilized, considering the murder of six million Jews, Soviet labor camps, or the barbarities of the Vietnam War.

The brutality of our freeways, megastructures, and skyscrapers; the increasing noise, violence, and pollution in our daily city life; the reckless depletion of natural resources—all are different expressions of the same phenomenon: Technology is no longer a means of enhancing civilized life, but a club to assert the violent propensities of our species, and human power over the rest of nature.

This new kind of "civilization"—which must be put in quotation marks—also shows signs of stress and malfunction. Witness the New York City blackout of 1977. It could still end with a bang.

But that is another, oft-told story. I hold that an urban and urbane civilization is within our grasp. In fact, we almost held it a century ago when flickering gas lights and clanking streetcars were just beginnning to provide new amenities.

The Victorian city has often been defamed, particularly by its own reformers, for the crowding of its tenements and the misery of its slums. We tend to deprecate the brilliance of Baron George Eugène Haussmann's Paris boulevards (to say nothing of his spanking sewer system), the elegance of Vienna's Ringstrasse, the *nouveau riche* grandeur of Berlin's Unter den Linden, the sparkle of Budapest's nightlife, or the simple pleasures of London's Hyde Park.

Today, we can and do appreciate all this again. Young people search the attics of old houses for the gimcrackery their parents had banned. They nail the old, hard-to-paint scrollwork back on the facade. Victorian furniture is suddenly valuable.

Only a few years ago, however, Victorian cities and buildings were universally considered a rank evil, the gimcrackery a crime, and the furniture oppressively gloomy. No one had anything good to say about cities whose light standards were supported by cast-iron lion paws and bare-breasted ladies.

Even Lewis Mumford, in his *The City in History,* ignored the unsurpassed civility of middle-class life in the great gas-lit cities and saw only the miseries of Coketown. He granted that automobile exhausts were worse than industrial coal dust, but he only grudgingly acknowledged that Haussmann, with his "bold and masterly treatment," along with the accomplishments of Sir Edwin Chadwick, Florence Nightingale, and Louis Pasteur, "robbed urban life at its lower level of some of its worst terrors and physical debasement."

Before the Victorians, city splendor had focused mainly on the royal palace and its gardens to keep the citizenry at a respectful distance. During Queen Victoria's reign, a growing, and increasingly prosperous, merchant middle class turned the cities of the industrialized Western world into a manifestation of its wealth and refinement. Most of the sewer systems and water works, public parks, botanical and zoological gardens, aquariums and planetariums, museums, concert halls, opera houses, city halls, central post offices, and court buildings— which sustain city life to this day—were built during what the Germans call the *Gründerjahre,* the founding years of modern capitalism, the years of the robber barons and their banking and industrial fiefs. The Eiffel Tower rose higher than the cathedrals. Railroad stations surpassed the grandeur of palaces. Twentieth-century technology, architecture, engineering, and ingenuity added little significance to urban life— except the mass-produced automobile and the ever-ringing telephone.

The sanitation technology of a century ago reduced urban stench and infant mortality. Boulevards were well lit, as were the sidestreets and alleys of the poor. Cheap, efficient transportation, mostly tramways, took everyone around the city and beyond to allotment gardens and country picnics.

Traffic was bad even then. Abundant amusement parks, vaudeville theaters, dance halls, parks and waterfronts with their boats for hire, open air concerts, beer gardens and coffee houses, were democratically frequented by the wide, social range of people who are today glued to their television sets. Our time has brought no communal improvements.

What may well have been the apogee of civilized city life was not confined to the great cities of Europe. The Baedeker of the United States, first published in 1893, and just recently reissued in a facsimile edition, lists such an abundance of city railroads, tramways, omnibuses, public carriages, and ferries that it makes one realize just how far backwards public transportation has traveled in this country. New York City's elevated railway, Baedeker says, ran at intervals of a few minutes during the day, and in a more or less continuous chain during rush hour. New York City, in 1893, made up for the absence of radio and television with 56 daily newspapers, 270 weekly papers and periodicals, and 350 monthly journals and magazines.

"Great injustice is done to Chicago," Baedeker says, "by those who represent it as wholly given over to the worship of Mammon, as it compares favorably with many American cities in the effort it has made to beautify itself by the creation of parks and boulevards and in its encouragement of education and the liberal arts. At present Chicago is exciting more than usual interest as the site of the Columbian exhibition [World's Columbian Exposition], celebrating the 400th anniversary of the discovery of America by Columbus."

The Columbian exhibition launched the City Beautiful movement, which, in turn, transformed the nation's capital and introduced the Parisian style of civic buildings and tree-lined boulevards in most American cities.

The glory lasted beyond the first world war. During the twenties, Detroit's assembly lines, economic dislocations, modern architecture, and city planning destroyed the efficient turn-of-the-century ambience.

As a child in the late 1920s and early 1930s in Berlin, for the price of a candy bar I would explore the city by trolley, the *Stadtbahn* (the electric circumferential railway), or the *U-Bahn* (the subway). No one thought it unusual that a six- or eight-year-old ventured out by himself to peek, a bit scared, through the beer smell and tobacco smoke of the working-class bars around Alexanderplatz, to daydream on the warm sand and pungent pine needles of Krumme Lanke, a sylvan suburb, or, to swim in Wannsee. I learned much about life, lying on Wannsee's man-made beach, watching long-legged girls and the vendors who sold pickled cucumbers.

In those days, the mailman rang twice daily at my mother's apartment and three times a day in the downtown business district. A letter within the city limits of Berlin, sent via the pneumatic tube that connected the city's post offices, was delivered within hours. Fresh rolls, milk, and eggs were delivered every morning along with the newspaper. Stores delivered your purchases. Doctors made house calls. While every family had a radio, only wealthy people had automobiles.

The deterioration of cities and city life in the last 50 years seems to be general throughout the Western world, but it is most pronounced in the United States. We have the means, and our government, according to the Supreme Court (*Berman* v. *Parker*), has the right to use its powers to keep our habitat "beautiful as well as clean, well-balanced as well as carefully patrolled."

But we did not have the will.

4   Automobility

What impedes our will to make cities beautiful, as well as clean, is our alleged infatuation with the automobile, a change in manufacturing techniques, and modern theories of city planning.

The fact that the automobile got the better of cities all over the world needs no elaboration. As David P. Billington, professor of engineering and architecture at Princeton, has said so succinctly, automobile dependency "disrupts life for both the city dweller, whose community structure crumbles, and the suburbanite, whose high mobility never settles down into a structured community at all."

The notion is still abroad, however, that Americans brought this dependency on themselves. It is said that we owe our entire lives, from conception to death, to our mechanical mistress; that in a fit of automania, we abandoned all public transportation. But that is at least partly a myth.

The demise of the streetcar, it now turns out, is not due to a broken heart. The auto industry broke its track. According to elaborate, little noticed, but well-documented testimony before the Senate Subcommittee on Antitrust and Monopoly in February 1973, General Motors contrived the death of 100 streetcar companies in 45 American cities.

According to chief witness Bradford C. Snell, the story began in 1925, when General Motors acquired the Yellow Coach

Company and began to manufacture buses. GM formed the Greyhound Corporation and a subsidiary named National City Lines.

Although motorists often cursed them, most tramway systems were doing well at the time. In 1936, in fact, streetcar manufacturers made a series of technical improvements that made streetcars more comfortable and popular. Several streetcar companies were owned by electric utilities until the Public Utility Holding Act of 1935 forced a separation.

Enter GM. Before anyone noticed, its subsidiary, National City Lines, bought the divested streetcar systems one after another and converted them to bus services. Then, our clever automakers sold the bus companies again, usually with the perhaps not inadvertent effect that the bus service deteriorated to the point where in most instances it was soon abolished. *C'est le capitalisme!*

Nowhere was the ruin from GM's motorization program more apparent than in southern California, said Snell. Los Angeles, a city of lush palm trees, fragrant orange groves, and ocean clean air, was served by the world's largest electric railway network. General Motors and allied highway interests arrived in the late 1930s. They bought the railway companies, scrapped the pollution-free electric trains, tore down their power transmission lines, ripped up their tracks, and placed GM buses on already congested Los Angeles streets. The noisy, foul-smelling buses drove patrons to automobile dealers, and millions of stalled motorists clamored for more freeways. The city of angels is an ecological wasteland. Palm trees are dying of petrochemical smog. Orange groves have been paved over by 300 miles of freeways. The air is now a septic tank into which four million cars, half of them built by General Motors, pump 13,000 tons of pollutants daily. Furthermore, a shortage of motor vehicle fuel and an absence of adequate public transport now threaten to disrupt the entire auto-dependent region.

Some people, like British architecture critic Reyner Banham, see a certain futuristic pop art charm in this chaos. It escapes me.

By 1949, Snell told the senators, "General Motors had replaced most trolley cars in the country with GM buses. In April of that year a Chicago federal jury convicted GM of having criminally conspired with Standard Oil of California, Firestone Tire, and others, to replace electric transportation with gasoline or diesel powered buses and to monopolize the sale of buses and related products to local transportation companies throughout the country. The court imposed a sanction of $5,000 on General Motors. In addition, the jury convicted H.C. Grossman, who was then Treasurer of General Motors. He was fined one dollar."

Next came the interstate "defense highway" system which, in 1956, well into the dawn of the atomic age, was sold to Congress on the theory of . . . what I am not really sure. Perhaps to evacuate our cities in the minutes that it takes nuclear missiles to cross the ocean (provided no stalled cars or fallen trees get in the way)? Or was it to move cannons across the country in the event we are invaded on both coasts (although mobile antimissile guns don't fit under our highway overpasses)?

At any event, the error of our "defense" highways in the city is now common knowledge. It is unlikely that many more will be built. A few might even be dismantled or at least placed underground. We are spending public money on improving and extending public transportation. We are looking for new ways to move people. The old trolley car may come back, for all is forgiven. Federal Department of Transportation officials are beginning to consider public transportation as what it should have been considered all along—a public utility as essential as

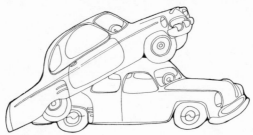

sewers and water. It is entirely possible that within the next decade or so public transportation will be free—wholly subsidized by the government. You already get a free ride on Seattle's downtown buses, and the benefits to the city (better business, reduced need for parking, less pollution, etc.) outweigh the costs by far.

Nor is this only a matter of commuting between downtown and the suburbs. The old charms of new suburbia are waning. Much of the city—jobs, stores, bars, restaurants, and entertainment—is moving into what used to be tranquil suburbs. The new "spread city" features commercial strips and strip tease, neon and noise, crime and congestion. Much of the old suburbia is in danger of turning into slums.

The problem, then, is to contain the spread and to assure orderly development. We no longer need transportation planning so much as we need what Victor Gruen called "anti-transportation planning." Transportation planning set out to make it easier to expand and urbanize even more open country. Antitransportation planning seeks to put things more closely together so people won't have to travel so far to get to where they need to go.

We are running out of gas.

5 Downtown

If urban amenity was run over by automobiles, the urban economy was crippled by fleeing factories. "I don't care about 150 Ph.d.'s moving out of Newark," Mayor Kenneth Gibson told Rep. Millicent Fenwick (R., N.J.). "But I weep for my breweries."

Roger Starr, New York City's leading housing expert, tells how he walked in a melancholic daze through the garment district, or what is left of it, "hoping to be knocked into by a young man pushing one of these handtrucks. It doesn't happen anymore because the young men have gone. Our garment industry depended on the ability to push a dress from the buttonhole maker to the button sewer, from the hem stitcher to the collar turner. They are all gone. They found it economically more efficient to produce it elsewhere."

There is no hope of luring the breweries back into Newark, the garment manufacturers back to New York City, the aircraft parts makers back to St. Louis, or the auto parts producers back to Detroit. They all progressed from manufacturing in the literal sense (Latin: *manus*, hand + *facere*, to make) to assembly line production. That means they need large amounts of land, which is cheaper out in the country, if indeed it is even available downtown. Since we let our railroads go to hell, industrial plants also need truck access, and downtown streets are

jammed. Besides, industry likes cheap labor and therefore tends
to run away from cities with strong unions.

Between 1954 and 1963, according to a government report,
the average American center city lost an average of 6,000
manufacturing plants, while out there, in spread city, some
14,000 new plants started humming. The exodus continues. It is
the same in all industrial cities around the world.

What is more, all around the world, farming has been
mechanized. The out of work farmhands have streamed into
the cities. But the jobs they look for have gone.

In the developing countries, these in-migrants build their
own miserable shanties in "belts of misery" around the city. In
highly industrialized countries like France and England, they
are settled outside the old cities near the new industrial parks.
In the United States, they have crowded into the inner city.
Luckily, as I mentioned earlier, farm mechanization in the
United States seems to have reached its apogee in recent years
and the in-migration seems to have stopped. But the cities have
not yet been able to put the newcomers to work.

What complicates matters is that in addition to the loss of
blue-collar work, white-collar office work is being automated.
While this has not caused a loss of jobs for those who have held
them all along, it prevents the creation of new jobs, although
business may be growing. The increased work is done by
computer. Besides, operating an electronic office machine is
hard to learn for a ghetto youngster who has not been taught to
read and write properly.

With employment and consequent poverty rampant in the
inner city, bankers drew a red line around the declining areas on
their secret maps, declared the areas a bad investment, and
refused to lend money for home improvements to any of the
people inside, whether or not they were willing and able to
repay their loans. Banks thus accelerated the deterioration of
the inner city until congressional investigations in the early
seventies called public attention to this "red-lining."

Private enterprise having made matters worse, the government was forced to step in and try to help. But government

programs, so far, have had only limited success, mostly because the programs have been so limited. Despite much noise about it, the federal government has given the cities only a fraction of the money it spends on farm subsidies. Nor have we ever had a consistent urban policy. Ever since the days of Franklin D. Roosevelt, the cities have been caught in a seesaw between liberals who wanted to build a better America in a hurry, and conservatives who want to keep America much as Norman Rockwell painted it on the covers of the *Saturday Evening Post*.

As soon as the liberals got a program going—public housing, urban renewal, new towns, rehabilitation, nonprofit moderate income housing built by churches or labor unions, urban homesteading, or whatnot—the conservatives tied it up in so many restrictions, regulations, and budget cuts that it never had a chance. Then the next administration would rush in and stop "the failure." It was always stop and go, stop and go.

Was urban renewal a failure? The program built some strong new downtown attractions—Boston's Government Center,

Philadelphia's Society Hill, Baltimore's Inner Harbor and Charles Center, to name but a few that strengthened their cities immeasurably. (What would have happened without them is obviously impossible to measure.)

The trouble was that Congress did not match downtown renewal with a vigorous public housing program. The old homes of the poor were bulldozed to make room for office buildings, luxury apartments, cultural centers, and all kinds of goodies except new homes for the poor. The blacks rightly called urban renewal "Negro removal," but were given no choice but to overcrowd other areas of the city. So in the end, we were only pushing the slums around. In the seventies, poverty and unemployment in the center cities was worse than in the sixties, according to a report by the National League of Cities.

By comparison, Canada, which has largely the same urban problems we have, never launched any massive federal programs. Except for the Trans-Canada Highway from British Columbia to Newfoundland, Canada never built multibillion-dollar national highways—freeways that would have carved up its cities. Instead, it spent the money to keep its railroads running smoothly. Canadian cities also kept their old streetcars and modernized them gradually. Toronto and Vancouver, as a consequence, are probably the most livable cities on this continent.

With more lucky inertia than clever foresight, the Canadians never got around to urban renewal until our mistakes became evident. A parliamentary task force reported that America's federal bulldozers did not, as expected, restore investor confidence in the inner city. Therefore, Parliament voted against wholesale slum clearance in 1969, but authorized national low-interest loans for housing rehabilitation and the improvement of public streets and sewers. This worked much better. As we approach the 1980s, this is just about where we find ourselves today.

We have done some perfectly wretched things downtown. Detroit's Renaissance Center, which looks like something from outer space—utterly unrelated to the city surrounding it—is one example. The "space age" Houston Center is equally inhuman, oversized, and alien. The nearby Greenway Plaza, another Houston megastructure, has at least a reminder of humanity: three children and an old man feeding pigeons. They are sculpted in bronze.

But we have live pigeons, too; and, what is more, an increasing number of little parks, plazas, and new benches where people can feed and enjoy the pigeons. We have rediscovered old buildings and old neighborhoods and are beginning to restore them and to put them to new use. We have more sidewalk cafes in our cities than we've ever had. People crowd museums, theaters, concert halls, and opera houses. There are more good restaurants, and not just fancy and expensive ones.

Just when it seemed that American cities, and with them, American civilization were doomed, there is a new urban optimism. In the last decade or so, as August Heckscher observed, "we have witnessed striking achievements by both the private and public sector in shaping a more hospitable urban environment. . . . A new understanding of urban amenities in the making."

This understanding includes an awareness that cities and civilization need continuity; that we cannot ignore history; that the city cannot be made over in some abstract, outer space image. It must be cared for like a garden—weeded, pruned, reseeded, and replanted—so that our cities and civilization can thrive.

Despite the Renaissance Centers, we are likely to see an urban renaissance in America. I do not, like Mayor Gibson of Newark, weep for the departed breweries and manufacturing plants. Good riddance. The city is merely changing functions. Rather than being an industrial center, it is becoming a managerial and cultural center, a place of learning and research, and a guardian of culture.

The change in function necessitates a change in the city's social structure. It has always been an anomaly peculiar to American cities that the poorest people should live on the most

expensive real estate—downtown, adjacent to the business and
cultural district. With the breweries gone, it is time that people
who need jobs in these breweries be given the opportunity to
follow them. We need policies to help people out of the ghetto
to where the jobs are. That will take a national urban growth
policy, which Congress asked for a decade ago, and which
Presidents Nixon and Ford, and so far President Carter as well,
have failed to produce.

The promise of a more hospitable urban environment, of an
urban renaissance, also includes a reexamination and redirec-
tion of architectural theory and practice. We need an
architecture and urban design that is human, as well as efficient,
mindful of historic continuity, as well as technically advanced.

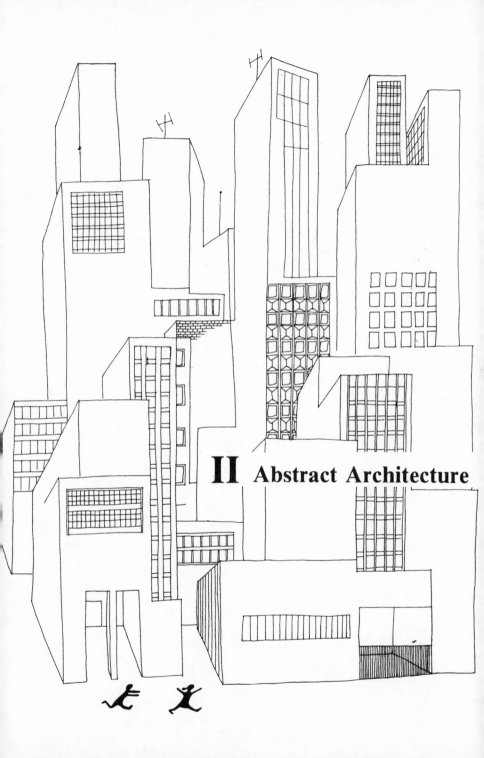

II Abstract Architecture

6   Premise and Promise

Each new art style gets its initial artistic fervor, not so much from the joy of creating something new, but from the *Schadenfreude*—the mischievous enjoyment of getting the better of the old. The Visigoths delighted in tearing down Roman temples. Gothic architects denounced and rebuilt Romanesque churches. The Renaissance thought Gothic positively barbaric, and so it goes.

John Steegman, who wrote a splendid book on *Victorian Taste*, asserts that "each age dislikes and derides the art and taste of its predecessors up to about a century preceding. The gentlemen of the 1760s threw out their Charles II furniture; the mid-Victorians banished their Chippendale to the servants' attics; in the 1930s everything later than the Regency was discarded."

Steegman must be right. We have just rediscovered the beauty and attendant virtues of buildings, artworks, and the aforementioned gimcrackery of 100 years ago. The artists of, say, 80 years ago, who pioneered the Modern movement, hated—yes, hated—late Victorian art and architecture with a polemic venom that sounds a little ridiculous today. They attacked the Victorian's establishment art and architecture—the academy—as degenerate, immoral, eclectic, derivative, and completely out of tune with the time and needs of people in the dawning machine age. They felt insulted by it.

In sum, the architectural revolution of the 1920s, like all revolutions, was more concerned with destroying the old order than creating a new one. It was a rebellion against the squalor of the industrial city, smothered, as the modern avant-garde saw it, in hypocritical, bourgeois bombast. Walter Gropius, one of the founders of the Modern movement, once told me that while watching a funeral procession in Berlin before World War I, he was so upset by the sight of the ornate coffin that he tracked down the undertaker and importuned him to strip this final shelter of the clutter of past ages. "The chaos of the time offended me," he said.

The first, rather self-conscious reaction to the Victorian mode was art nouveau, a style that had no particular *Weltanschauung* except, perhaps, a melancholy sensuality that draped everything, from building facades to ink wells, in limpid vegetation and equally limpid female nudes.

But that was, if anything, even more degenerate than Victorian. And while it served the needs of people in the dawning machine age fairly well—art nouveau made extensive use of cast iron, and many of its objects were made by machine—it did not *express* the modern sunrise.

To expose Victorian clutter and wickedness, modern architects wanted clean lines and clean living, up high, in sunshine and fresh air. They wanted "honest" structures, clearly expressed. They were possessed by a giddy idolatry of machinery and the promise of what mass production might do for the masses.

Now that had never occurred to the Victorians. They looked at machines as tools for making things. The Modernists said buildings should be machines—machines to live in—or else they should *look* like machines.

Although it was all intended to be architecture for the people, modern architecture was never any more popular than modern art. Like most modern art, it is perpetually up front with its avant-garde, but never brings up the rear.

This turned out to be disastrous for our environment.

In the past it would not have mattered much. Architects

would work only for prelates, princes, and potentates, occasionally also designing the rampart of a town or the vistas of a city. The environment of the people was built by the people. Artisans helped, of course, But everything was built on instinct and tradition. People used natural materials, readily at hand, making the most of location on the site and orientation to sun and wind. As Socrates had enjoined, people would take care to build pleasant places to live and safe places to store one's belongings, cool in the summer and warm in the winter. Architecture without architects, as you still find it around the New England commons, Alpine villages, or Mediterranean hilltowns, is invariably beautiful and functional.

Folk architecture, however, went the way of the spinning wheel. The skill withered and the instinct blurred, and so did the innate sense of beauty. People feel lost and unsure of themselves in a habitat not of their own making.

In 1923, Le Corbusier, another founder of the Modern movement, declared in *Vers Une Architecture*, the canon of modern architecture, that in the machine age, "the human animal stands breathless and panting before a tool that he cannot take hold of. Progress appears to him as hateful as it is praiseworthy. All is confusion within his mind. He feels himself to be the slave of a frantic state of things and experiences no sense of liberation or comfort . . ."

Le Corbusier said, in effect: calm yourself, human animal. We shall create a new architecture to take care of you. We shall no longer design only cathedrals and palaces for prelates, princes and potentates. Instead, we shall design the healthy and efficient *machine à habiter*—the mechanized, mass-produced house and habitat—for everyone.

"It will rise one day toward heaven from the hands of a million workers like the crystal symbol of a new faith," chimed in Walter Gropius, when he founded the Bauhaus.

"Architecture or Revolution!" shouted Le Corbusier.

What he meant, I gather, was that the industrial age had corrupted and polluted the habitat that folk architecture had built. The corruption and pollution were detrimental to public health and welfare, and people would surely not tolerate it for long. To avoid a popular uprising, Le Corbusier and friends proposed that a new breed of architects take matters in hand, create an industrial architecture, and with it, "a total man-made environment."

Gropius frequently used this phrase, and "the total man-made environment" keeps coming up when architects get together. It makes me uneasy.

On the one hand, since *someone* must design the products of industrial mechanization and specialization, it makes sense that he be an artist who sees to it that things are well designed and harmoniously constructed. I like order and believe designers should design with the "total man-made environment" in mind.

On the other hand, total design for total perfection easily becomes totalitarian. Total design does not often dare risk freedom and individual creativity. The residents in Mies van der Rohe's Lake Shore Drive Apartments in Chicago, for instance, may not hang curtains of their own choosing. That would spoil the total environment. In Eero Saarinen's CBS

Building in New York, even high-level executives may not change their waste baskets or ashtrays, let alone the paintings on their walls. The corporate image permits no individualism.

Le Corbusier recognized that creating total architecture to avoid chaos and revolution would require more than practicing traditional architectural techniques. There must first be "a revolution in the conception of what architecture is," he said. It is to advance social purposes.

This conception did not long endure beyond lip service and manifestos. Le Corbusier himself was among the first avant-gardists to become discouraged with social projects and return to chapels and palaces.

Some historians argue that modern architecture began before Gropius and Le Corbusier with the use of machine-made materials in Joseph Paxton's Crystal Palace for the London Exhibition of 1851, or the steel frame and curtain wall construction in William Le Baron Jenney's Home Insurance Company Skyscraper, first seen in Chicago in 1883. Aesthetically, modern architecture began with the twentieth-century work of Frank Lloyd Wright in the United States and H. P. Berlage in the Netherlands.

Paxton and Jenny, Wright and Berlage, however, did not

share the messianic *Weltanschauung* that burst forth in Paris, Weimar, and Berlin in the early 1920s—in Le Corbusier's atelier on the ground floor of a Jesuit cloister at the Rue de Sèvres; in Walter Gropius's Bauhaus in the old *Kunst-gewerbeschule*, or arts and crafts school; and on the pages of Mies van der Rohe's art magazine *G* (for *Gestaltung*). Mies succeeded Gropius as Bauhaus director in 1930, after its move from Weimar to Dessau.

As these three pioneers saw it—and as I use the term in this book—modern architecture claims to be more than the art and science of designing buildings. It includes the design of "the total man-made environment"—building, interior, furniture, industrial, urban, and landscape design. Le Corbusier, Mies van der Rohe, and Gropius practiced all these, and so do their followers.

Architecture, declared the members of the *Congrés Interna-tionaux d'Architecture Moderne* (CIAM), "is the key to every-thing. Architecture presides over the destinies of the city."

The notion that architecture was the key not only to peoples' betterment but also to better people was inherited from the English arts and crafts movement of John Ruskin and William Morris. "Architecture," said Ruskin in 1849, "is the art which so disposes and adorns the edifices raised by man, for whatsoever uses, that the sight of them may contribute to his mental health, power, and pleasure." Morris added in 1880 that "the glorious art of architecture, now for some time slain by commercial greed . . . will so quicken our vision that it will outrun the slow lapse of time, and show us the victorious days when millions of those who now sit in darkness will be enlightened by an Art made by the people and for the people."

There was but one fundamental difference between the two evangelist design movements. Morris's millions were to conquer the evils of the industrial age by returning to medieval crafts. Gropius's millions would make their "crystal symbol" by machine, and conquer the evils by reconciling art and industry. While the nineteenth-century arts and crafts movement rejected technology, the twentieth-century Modernists would marry it.

In their zeal, the Modernists swore to renounce all bonds to the past, snipping even the most tenuous ties of old flirtations. "History," they said, "is bunk." It was not until a few years ago that American architecture schools resumed teaching history.

The trouble with the attempt to give buildings a machine-made look was that nobody could tell for sure how a machine-made building was supposed to look. Machines can only make things that people design. So the architects had to find design inspiration. And since that inspiration could not be associated with the past, they went, not to engineers, but—to painters.

7 Abstract Constructions

Painters have always depicted architecture. In the Modern movement, architects set out to create three-dimensional paintings.

Modern architects found the forms to follow the functions of their architecture in the canvasses of Picasso, Mondrian, Malevich, and other abstract painters; in the art and giddy theorizing of French Cubism, Italian Futurism, Dutch de Stijl, and Soviet Constructivism. In fact, we learned of the full extent of the Constructivist influence only in recent years, as Soviet officials opened their archives and collections.

"Painting became the transfer point of architecture," declared one of the leading Constructivists, El Lissitzky. Le

Corbusier transferred at lunch. He would paint in the morning, and practice architecture in the afternoon.

The foremost inspiration for the white cubes of early modern architecture came from the beige cubes painted by Picasso, Braque, Juan Gris, Marcel Duchamp, and Fernand Léger before World War I. Cubism, as explained by Sigfried Giedion, the art historian and chief propagandist of the Modern movement, broke with Renaissance perspective to view objects relatively, that is, simultaneously from several points of view. To the three dimensions of the Renaissance, Giedion says, the Cubists and modern architecture added a fourth one—time. He entitled his most important book *Space, Time and Architecture,* and asserts that modern painters and architects intuitively felt the import of Einstein's theories. It must have been intuition since artists were not likely to have read, let alone understood, Einstein's *Elektrodynamik bewegter Körper,* his first thesis, published in 1905.

Gropius, Mies, and Le Corbusier, each in his own way, started by designing Cubist images—buildings that consisted of interlocking cubes of various sizes. With the addition of glass walls they seemed to have added a fourth dimension because of the possibility of simultaneous views of the inside and outside of a building (unless someone draws a curtain, of course).

Modern architects were extraordinarily proud of this "indoor-outdoor" relationship that they saw as a rebuke to the Victorian obsession with womb-like enclosures. It is indeed attractive to be in a room that seems part of a garden or some other pleasant view. But views are expensive. Picture windows without pictures are part of the modern malaise.

Even in my younger days, when I swallowed Giedion's gospel whole, I had difficulty seeing Gropius's Fagus factory—a dour building in East Germany—move like Duchamp's "Nude Descending the Staircase."

Mondrian, Theo van Doesburg, and their de Stijl group, with its jarringly asymmetrical play of lines and planes in primary colors, contributed another mode to modernity. Van Doesburg was a painter, man of letters, and architect who hoped to

convert architecture into "pure art." He also wanted to introduce Bauhaus students to his theories, but Gropius refused to admit him to the school. Van Doesburg came anyway and held classes in a nearby Weimar inn. His illicit influence was all the stronger.

The most prophetic art group that inspired the Modernists was the Italian Futurists. Poets, painters, sculptors, and architects sought to liberate art from its age-old aim of permanence and make it a thing of the moment. "We affirm that the splendor of the world has been enriched by a new beauty: the beauty of speed," the Futurists declared in 1909. They were enamored of "vibrations."

One of the group, Antonio Sant'Elia, invented fantastic cityscapes. His "Citta Nuova," exhibited in Milan in 1914, expressed this infatuation with skyscrapers pierced and entwined by freeway ramps, overpasses and underpasses, subways, and exterior elevators. It was to be elastic and light, built of steel, concrete, and chemically treated paper.

Sant'Elia died two years after the show. But his influence on Le Corbusier's *Ville Radieuse* was as profound as the influence of *La Ville Radieuse* upon our cities today. Wherever we go in the modern world, we see clusters of widely spaced high-rise slabs, monotonous and forbidding, like brobdingnagian tombstones.

The Bauhaus was a laboratory of art and industrial design that radically changed art education and launched what became the establishment style for "everything from the coffee cup to city planning," as Mies van der Rohe put it. (Actually, modern was not to be a "style." That was a dirty word at the Rue de Sèvres and the Bauhaus. Design was to be a matter of rational "problem solving." The marriage of artistic genius and technical production was to bring forth pure form, following pure function, with not a hint of adornment.)But the Bauhaus practiced and taught little architecture.The notion that there is a Bauhaus architecture is based on the Bauhaus Building in Dessau, which Gropius designed in 1925, and the private work of such Bauhaus teachers as Gropius himself, Mies, and Marcel Breuer. The Bauhaus painters—all Abstract Expressionists— were surely equally important.

Paul Klee taught painting and the metal workshop. Kandinsky taught stained glass. Feininger was in charge of the printing shop. Josef Albers took over the mandatory "basic course" from Johannes Itten. Itten called the course "the big house-cleaning of the mind." The students called it "purgatory."

The most influential artist at the Bauhaus, I would say, was Laszlo Moholy-Nagy. He converted the energy of the Bauhaus into usable design, the best-selling Bauhaus item being wallpaper. Moholy was born in Hungary, where he had learned about Russian Constructivism.

The Constructivists—a few of whom also called themselves Suprematists—were members of the "Soviet Union of Contemporary Architects," founded in 1925. They became the dominant art faction in the Soviet Union in the brief period between Lenin's NEP (New Economic Order) and Stalin's assumption of power, that is, between 1928 and 1931. The big names—most of them painters, sculptors, architects, philosophers, and utopians all at once—include Vladimir Tatlin, Naum Gabo, Antoine Pevsner, El Lissitzky, Konstantin

Melnikov, and the three brothers Alexander, Leonid, and Viktor Vesnin. Until he left the Soviet Union, Marc Chagall was also a member.

The Constructivists considered themselves part of an "international front of contemporary architecture." In 1927, the board of coworkers included such non-Russians as Walter Gropius, Mies van der Rohe, and eventually, Le Corbusier, along with lesser luminaries from Belgium and Poland. The Constructivists also considered themselves "shapers of life" and "appointed builders of socialism." Their dreams and rhetoric were much the same as that of the Western avant-garde—and so was their art and architecture. It is hard to tell which is chicken or which is egg, and I doubt that the chicken omelette can ever be unscrambled.

But until recently, relatively little was known about Constructivist work and workings. Stalin not only repressed the group's creative enthusiasm, but the memory of it as well. All we had seen of Russia's "lost avant-garde," as someone called it, were poor reproductions of poor reproductions of the same old illustrations in the architecture history books: Tatlin's leaning tower, memorializing the Third Internationale, or the Vesnin brothers' glass cage design for the Leningrad Pravda Building.

We knew that the Soviets sent several Constructivist exhibitions to Europe—to Berlin in 1922, Cologne in 1928, and Paris in 1937—usually accompanied by El Lissitzky, who had studied in Darmstadt and had many friends among the German avant-garde. Many German and Swiss architects and planners, in turn, helped the Soviets build their new towns. Le Corbusier designed one building in Moscow and then went home mad because he failed to win the international competition for the Palace of Soviets. He was not a good loser.

Giedion does not tell us much about the Russians. Smarting under Nazi denunciations of their alleged *Kultur-Bolschewismus,* Giedion and the people he wrote about saw no reason to admit to red sheep in the family. Nor was there any reason for Gropius, Mies, Moholy-Nagy, Marcel Breuer, Josef Albers, Herbert Bayer, and other Bauhaus artists to brag about their relation to Soviet culture after they escaped from the Nazis to America.

Recently, however, other books began to appear, and in 1971, the Hayward Gallery in London presented a superb exhibition of Constructivist design, later shown in the New York Cultural Center. It was like walking into a Bauhaus exhibit with Russian labels. There was, it appeared, little difference between *"proletkult"* (the Russian code word), and *"Gesamtkultur,"* or "the total man-made environment" as conceived in the 1920s.

You could see the same awkward, uncomfortable early Bauhaus wood furniture; the same bicycle handle bars bent into chairs; the same workers' overalls; the same white, machine-for-living houses; the same ceramic and hammered metal utensils; the same glass enclosed circular staircases; the same typography of extra-bold, sans serif type with fat black bars and big red circles.

The Constructivist buildings were bizarre. Nikolai Ladovskii drew a suspended restaurant, to be supported, as I understand it, by light beams. El Lissitzky designed what he called a "Proun Room" (the word is of his own invention), which attempts to create "the ultimate illusion of irrational space" and destroys the illusion modern museums treat us to that recent spatial experiments are a new idea.

Lissitzky also designed what he called "cloud presses": skyscrapers in the shape of a T. The towers, which house elevators, support huge slabs, which house people. This concept is echoed 40 years later in buildings by the Japanese architect Kenzo Tange. In an apparent effort to "modernize" Japan's people and traditions, Tange likes to design clumsy concrete conglomerations of large-scale and massive monumentality. Ivan Leonidov designed a Lenin Institute that was to consist of a glazed library tower for 15,000 books and an elevated spherical auditorium for 40,000 people, all connected to the city center by monorail. One of the few schemes that was actually built was Melnikov's Rusakov Club for a labor union in Moscow. It bears a striking resemblance to Marcel Breuer's Whitney Museum in New York, built in 1966.

Like those held by CIAM colleagues in the West, the Soviet Constructivist debates focused on building society and its cities. There was, first of all, the family. Lenin would liberate woman from household drudgery which, he said, drives her "to the brink of madness with its unproductive, soul-destroying, energy-sapping trivialities." Soviet architects therefore made plans for dormitories with communal kitchens. Social life was to take place in workers' clubs—"social condensers," they were called—where people were to be transformed from egocentric materialists to idealistic socialists. Children were to be raised in state institutions, an idea that the 1931 Communist Party Congress officially abandoned.

The biggest dispute was between the "urbanists" and the "disurbanists." The urbanists wanted to preserve the old cities, spruce them up with more greenery, and accommodate their surplus population in carefully planned satellite towns. The disurbanists proposed to carry out Lenin's instruction to eliminate inequalities between city life and rural life by abolishing cities altogether. Abundant generation of electric power and what the Russians called "Fordizatsiia" (Henry Ford's assembly-line mass production) would make it unnecessary to concentrate science and culture. (Prominent American city planners more recently said the same about electronic communication.) Human life, the Soviet disurbanists said, could now be spread across the countryside along highways and electric power lines.

As solved by one leading disurbanist, Nikolai Aleksandrovich Miliutin, town and country would merge in one endless urban belt, consisting of parallel transportation, and industrial, recreational, residential, and agricultural ribbons. Schemes for similar "linear cities" have been proposed before and are reinvented again and again. (But no one invented the ones we actually built in the United States—without plan and in a distressingly messy way. We call them "strip developments.")

The urbanist-disurbanist debate was abruptly silenced by Stalin, an old-fashioned urbanist with a taste for muscular statuary on gingerbread palaces. According to S. Frederick Starr, a leading historian of Soviet culture, Stalin also denounced the Constructivists as bourgeois aesthetes, insufficiently conversant with Marxism, partisan to utilitarian "machine fetishism," and scarcely distinguishable from American engineers. Mies, in a meeting in Moscow, assured his Soviet Colleagues that contemporary architecture was under attack everywhere. It could only be saved, he said, by a "state dictatorship" that would champion its cause.

As it turned out, the Nazi state dictatorship would not champion his cause, and he immigrated to America. The true champions of modern architecture turned out to be capitalist corporations.

East and West wings of the modern avant-garde differed mostly in the status they enjoyed. For a short spell, the Constructivists held power in Russia, while the Bauhaus was scarcely known or taken seriously by the German public. Le Corbusier kept complaining about the indifference of the French.

East and West, times were terrible and little was being built, although after 1926, the Soviet Union started construction of literally hundreds of new towns and industrial settlements in successive five-year plans.

Lacking commissions, architects like to busy themselves with utopian schemes and debates. The schemes tend to be abstract. It is easy to forget people when there aren't any around to object or ask questions about cost, structural feasibility, and how the thing fits into daily life.

In 1932, when Henry-Russell Hitchcock and Philip Johnson took stock of the accomplishments of the Modern movement, they called it the International Style, in a book of that name. They might also have called it the Style of the International. But since Stalin had suppressed the Soviet contribution by that time, Hitchcock and Johnson knew little about it.

At any event, neither "Modern" nor "International Style" adequately denotes the style of architecture that emerged. Any art style is modern when it first appears, and most art styles cross national borders.

The proper name is abstract architecture.

8   Ornament

The chief characteristic of abstract architecture is the absence of ornament.

Ornament was declared "a crime" by the Viennese architect Adolf Loos, who got discouraged by the sensuous decadence of art nouveau and railed against it in an essay entitled "Ornament and Crime," published in 1908.

It seems likely that Loos got the idea from Louis Sullivan, a grandfather of modern architecture, whom Loos met on a trip to America where he washed dishes and admired skyscrapers. In 1892, the year before Loos's visit, Sullivan had written that "it would be greatly for our aesthetic good, if we could refrain entirely from the use of ornament for a period in order that our thought might concentrate acutely upon the production of buildings well formed and comely in the nude."

Sullivan's own buildings were well formed and comely. Nude they were not. Sullivan decorated them with ornaments of his own invention, as rich and intricate as anything since the Persians.

Loos, however, had returned to the Vienna of Sigmund Freud and decided that ornament was undoubtedly of erotic origin. Consider the cross. When caveman first drew a horizontal line on the wall, Loos wrote, he meant to depict woman. Then he drew a vertical line through the horizontal and that showed man penetrating her. Any questions?

Loos apparently had also read Karl Marx, because he further asserted that ornament "is a crime against the national economy . . . it is wasted labor and hence wasted wealth." He deduced this from the fact that embroiderers and lacemakers were paid low wages. Ergo, he reasoned without compelling logic, the absence of ornament would mean "shorter working hours and consequently higher wages." The thrust of his argument was that "lack of ornament is a sign of spiritual strength."

That launched the age of architectural nudism.

No one, except exhibitionists, was happy with it—not for long. It was clearly a case of the emperor's new clothes. Loos himself kept adorning his buildings with moldings, decorative columns and paneling. Only toward the end of his career did he stop this criminal conduct to design a few naked houses. He also recanted.

He had "freed humanity from *unnecessary* ornament," he wrote in the 1930s. "Twenty-six years ago, I maintained that ornament would disappear from articles of use as man develops . . . I never meant that decorations should be ruthlessly and systematically done away with . . . Only when time has made it disappear, can it ever be applied again, just as man will never go back to tattooing his face."

Won't he, Herr Loos? Tattooing is the rage again. People in our society don't tattoo their faces, perhaps, having mustaches and artificial eyelashes for decoration. But people in growing numbers tattoo their chests, breasts, buttocks, and other parts

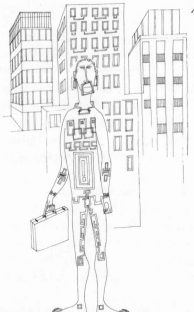

of their anatomy. And they no longer do so with only the nautical, erotic, and patriotic symbols that sailors and longshoremen traditionally used for body decoration. The new fad employs multicolored, stylized images of the mystic cultism that is spreading across the country. And on their bodies you find the same monsters, dervishes, and astrological signs you see airbrushed on cars and vans.

Whatever else the tattooing, decorating of automobiles, and subway graffiti might mean, they are evidence that the urge for ornament is irrepressible. It is under people's skin, as it were. Who is Adolf Loos to tell us that it is a crime and bad taste?

Under this code of artistic judgment, no woman (or man, for that matter) could ever wear a floral print and we would have to stop icing our cakes. What is more, even the modern elite have been cheating all along, putting Persian rugs under their Breuer chairs, and richly ornamented antiques against their white- and light-washed walls. Mies himself lived in a Victorian apartment house.

Having sold themselves on nude virtue, the Modernists would not retreat. They met the urge for ornament by turning entire buildings into something ornamental, into megasculptures, into the abstraction of "exciting spaces," into form for form's sake.

Social purpose was quickly forgotten. It was *l'architecture pour l'architecture*—with a vengeance. One critic, with subconscious irony, called the leading twentieth-century architects "form-givers."

Mies was the first to see modern architecture not as a tool of social reform, but as abstract ornament. He combined slabs of differently colored marble, chromed steel beams, precious wood, a pool of water, beautifully placed sculpture, into an exquisitely proportioned composition. His first great building—the one that made him famous—served no purpose whatsoever. It was the German pavilion at the 1929 International Exhibition in Barcelona and there was nothing in it but that famous chair. After all, the King of Spain might drop by and wish to sit down. Architecture or Revolution!

Le Corbusier tinkered with his "machines to live in" some years longer. But one day in 1950, impulsively and without warning, he gave up the struggle for an architectural formula that might help or house people and bring rampant technology under control. He created Ronchamp, a small chapel in the Vosges Mountains that separate France from Germany.

Ronchamp is a work of abstract sculpture—emotion in concrete. Le Corbusier himself called it "not a building, but a monument." It is not architecture for worship so much as a shrine for the worship of architecture. And worshiped it was—

RONCHAMP

by critics, curators, experts, connoisseurs, and teachers of architecture around the world. From Ronchamp on, the Modern movement has been schizophrenic.

The classic wing coasts on Mies' philosophy that "less is more." Mies finally reduced his Gallery of Twentieth Century Art in Berlin to a roof with four pillars, covering an invisible, glass-enclosed space. It is architecture reduced to the absurd, much as Malevich, with his "White on White" canvas, reduced painting *ad absurdum*.

The romantic wing glides on Le Corbusier's bon mot that "architecture is the masterly, correct and magnificent play of masses brought together in light." At Ronchamp, Chandigarh, Harvard, and other places, he gave us buildings as complex and tortured as Picasso's "Guernica." Remote from the lives of people who pass them, and even the people who worship, work, and study within, these buildings, like those of Mies, are nonobjective works of art. They are not social art. They further confuse that human animal.

Le Corbusier's free-form romanticism was anticipated by more than three decades by Eric Mendelsohn's Einstein Tower at Potsdam. It was an astrological observatory that pleased Albert Einstein but baffled most other people. From this somewhat eccentric work of expressionist architecture, Mendelsohn went on to an expression of purpose in such practical buildings as department stores, movie houses, and corporate headquarters.

Mendelsohn, who considered himself a thoroughly modern architect, never used ornament. Neither did he turn his buildings into ornamental sculpture. Instead, he combined romantic flair with functional restraint and used elements of his buildings in joyfully ornamental ways—a swervingly rounded corner, a spiraling staircase, a ribbon of windows wrapped around his facade.

His architecture was a popular success. He had the largest and busiest architectural office in Europe before Hitler forced him to flee, first to what was then Palestine, where he designed the University Medical Center on Mount Scopus in Jerusalem, then to the United States, where he designed a number of noted synagogues.

Mendelsohn is not mentioned in the official propaganda histories of the Modern movement. There is not a word on him in Nikolaus Pevsner's *Pioneers of Modern Design*, published in 1936. Nor does he even rate a footnote in Giedion's frequently revised text, first published in 1941.

The architectural fantasies Eric Mendelsohn sketched as a soldier in World War I were prophetic visions of structures built almost half a century later. Examples are the Dulles airport terminal, the Air Force Academy chapel, and the Watergate office and apartment house complex in Washington, D.C. But the orthodox Abstractionists rejected Mendelsohn's architecture as romantic and "expressionist." For them, the heretic simply did not exist.

Not only ornament was suspect. Even likable architecture was denounced and ignored.

9 Slab-Space-Slab

In August 1933, the modern avant-gardes from many countries joined for a Mediterranean cruise that left from Marseilles and stopped for a week in Athens. It was the fourth meeting of CIAM.

The group included Gropius, Mies, Marcel Breuer, Moholy-Nagy from Germany, the French painter Fernand Léger, art critic Sigfried Giedion from Switzerland, Alvar Aalto from Finland, Richard Neutra from the United States, Cornelius Van Eesteren from Holland, José Luis Sert from Spain, and other architects, artists, scientists, and their companions. CIAM was founded a few years earlier in the chateau of Helene de Mandrot at La Sarraz, Switzerland, essentially in protest against the architectural jury that failed to award first prize to Le Corbusier in the international competition for a new League of Nations building in Geneva. CIAM remained dominated by Le Corbusier and his ideas and soon dominated urban design around the world.

As they had at CIAM-1, 2, and 3, the cruising group not only talked, joked, debated, and lectured one another with boisterous intensity, but they also issued grandiloquent declarations and manifestos. Ten years later, in the desolation of occupied Paris, Le Corbusier anonymously published these resolutions under the title of *The Athens Charter*. The book is introduced with an obtuse essay by playwright Jean

Giraudoux, the author of *Tiger at the Gates* and *The Madwoman of Chaillot*. I suppose Giraudoux's purpose was to confuse the Gestapo. None of Le Corbusier's many admiring biographers, at any rate, explain the circumstances of this publication, unavailable in English until 1973, with a subsequent introduction by Sert. By that time, the book had only historic interest. CIAM wisdom had become conventional.

Hitler unwittingly helped spread this wisdom as he helped spread all modern art, because he forced modern and liberal artists and intellectuals into exile. Along with Gropius (and later, Sert) at Harvard, Mies at the Illinois Institute of Technology, Moholy-Nagy at the Chicago Bauhaus, and other avant-garde designers at other schools, CIAM concepts were introduced throughout the free world long before *The Athens Charter* was obscurely published. The modern style and *Weltanschauung* quietly occupied all the strategic points of art and architectural education. When the war was over, a new generation of architects and planners was ready to rebuild the world in CIAM's modern image.

The goal of CIAM, as stated by Le Corbusier, was a belief in "a truly human architecture. . . . which, pursuant to climates, customs, and races, allows for every diversity of form, but submits each of them to. . . . a sound notion of the human scale, and a profound respect for individuality."

The charter's specifics are, for the most part, as noble and unassailable as these goals. We are told at length that the problems of the center city can only be solved in the context of the surrounding urban region, but that coordinated city and regional planning is hampered because urban development rarely coincides with political jurisdictions. Planners are urged to take into account such environmental factors as land, water, vegetation, climate, economics, politics, and historic traditions. They are cautioned to be prepared for constant change. All residents should be assured by law of *"les joies essentielles,"* the essential joys of urban life.

In Le Corbusier's bombastic and redundant language, the

charter also calls for adequate open space for recreation, preservation of historic buildings and sites, and strict separation of pedestrians and motor vehicles—gospels that were farsighted at the time, and that are as commonplace and ignored today as the gospel of Brotherly Love.

It is mainly the rigid, almost fanatic application of the gospel that led CIAM city planning astray. The central thrust of the charter's doctrine was ubiquitously and disastrously taken to heart by planners, developers, and politicians. It stems from the concern of CIAM and all other urbanists over the "chaos" that entered the city with the dislocations and sense of homelessness caused by mechanization. The worst manifestation of this chaos, the charter declares, is the overcrowding of the old city centers with as many as 400 and even 600 inhabitants per acre. Combined with poverty—such crowding has led to slums, disastrous housing conditions, diseases, crime, and deprivation. The growth of the city, furthermore, devours the surrounding green space and thus further removes the slum dweller from ready access to nature and health.

Ebenezer Howard, who led the British Garden City movement, which was the only counterforce to CIAM (and was badly on the defensive, at that), proposed to attack this problem by building "garden cities." These were satellite towns placed in a "greenbelt" that surrounds the old city, each connected to one another by fast trains. The new towns, cooperatively built, would lure people out of the slums by offering not only attractive homes and gardens, but employment, education, and recreation as well. Howard saw his towns as "social cities." The vacated slums would be torn down and replaced by parks to make the big cities more livable again. London always remained the central focus of Howard's concern.

The Athens Charter called this proposal "a generous movement. . . .to release men from the inhumanity of the modern city." But it asserted that Howard and his followers regarded the single-family house as the sole remedy for urban ills (which they did not) and that therefore, "unhappily, this solution leads to a scattering of dwellings and to the complete alienation of certain inhabited areas."

Elsewhere, Le Corbusier said that the Garden City idea presents a danger of "deurbanization" and "a sterile isolation of the individual," who would be kept in "a slavery organized by capitalist society." (Many, if not most, of Howard's followers, were Fabian socialists.)

The aim of *The Athens Charter,* in contrast, was not the alleged dispersal of the city, but rather "the aeration of the city."

Aeration, the charter says, was to be accomplished by tearing down the slums and housing their residents in high-rise buildings spaced far apart, so that each tower would be immersed in sunshine and fresh air and command a fine view. The open space between towers was to be traversed by high-speed freeways, planted with greenery, and provided with "all the social organizations that lighten the task of the mistress of the house and the mother of the family," such as daycare centers, schools, and playgrounds.

This was to be "the city designed for speed." It was the city in which various functions of life were to be segregated into various zones. It was *La Ville Radieuse,* the radiant machine-made city, which followed Le Corbusier's vain pursuit of the machine house. As Le Corbusier correctly asserted in the charter, it became the key to abstract architecture.

The Radiant City, first exhibited in 1930, is the culmination of Le Corbusier's urban designs, the epitome of his life's work, and the essence of his contribution. It was a theoretical project consisting of a series of drawings, sketches and theorems that he presented in various forms at various times, and on which he worked intermittently beginning in 1922. The Radiant City assimilates several urban design and city planning theories, including those of Ebenezer Howard, the Austrian Camillo Sitte, the German *Siedlungen* of the Werkbund, the *Nuova Citta* of Italian Futurists, and the linear city of the Soviet Constructivists.

The first basic element is the high-rise apartment house that Le Corbusier designed for several heights and in various forms—as towers and slabs, with a cruciform floor plan. At one time he argued that apartment houses should never be higher than eight double stories, so that people living on the top could still feel close to the trees outside. "The miracle of trees and parks," Le Corbusier said, would keep the city in the human scale and people in contact with nature.

At other times, Le Corbusier wanted skyscrapers 65-stories high, on the theory that the vertical concentration of people would free more spaces for parks. In one of his projects he houses 1,000 people on 2½ acres, but covers only 12 percent of his land with buildings. This "vertical garden city," Le Corbusier wrote, "will turn the joys of nature into a daily occurrence and not merely an optional Sunday pleasure."

This extreme aeration, Le Corbusier argued, was the only method to restore unity of scale to urban life. However, he was often bothered by the question of whether his huge dimensions could be adapted to humans, or whether they would frighten

and alienate people. "In providing for vast empty spaces in this imaginary city, dominated everywhere by the overspreading sky," he said, "I was very much afraid that these empty spaces might be 'dead,' that boredom might reign and panic seize the people living there." But he never did anything about it.

A second basic element of the Radiant City is the elimination of the street as an intimate social space, as an important stage setting for the human drama. The charter declared the distances between typical street intersections as much too short and much too hard on automobiles, which must slow down—poor things—or even stop before they reach full gear. Instead of the street where people meet, loiter, gossip, watch and protect one another, where children play, and where a sense of neighborhood develops—the Modern movement gave us the super-block, traversed by super-wide motor roads and dominated by vast open spaces, most of them used for parking rather than parks, unless covered by mangy grass and "keep off" signs. If the street dies, the city dies.

A third basic tenet of Le Corbusier's ideal city is rigidly segregated organization. In all his plans, before the Radiant City and after, Le Corbusier indicates clearly defined districts for housing, hotels, embassies, businesses, factories and warehouses, heavy industry, and so forth. His motor road networks became a highway engineer's dream with high-speed lanes, slow-moving lanes, local lanes, underpasses, overpasses, and pedestrian walks. While the highway engineers gave us a sticky mess of spaghetti, however, Le Corbusier's transportation plans serve the spaghetti straight and uncooked. There is no allowance even for the possibility of a hill, or a river, or a view, or human boredom. Nor did Le Corbusier or *The Athens Charter* consider any mode of transportation other than the automobile—an automobile, furthermore, in constant motion. Only a few of Le Corbusier's urban designs allow cars to stop and park.

The theoretical diagram of the Radiant City and its procrustean aesthetics weren't the only problems with the charter. Far worse was the CIAM concept used to destroy parts of our old cities. In pure form it was applied only once to an entire city—Brasilia, the new capital of Brazil. I found it a nightmare. There are also some new districts adjoining old cities built in the Radiant City image. One is La Defense, beyond the Arc de Triomphe in Paris. Others are New Zagreb and New Bucharest. All are, I think, forever doomed to be their own mausoleums.

The real horror, however, was CIAM's idea of the "renovation" of cities, or urban renewal. Urged by *The Athens Charter,* it has come to mean replacing the lively, organic complexity of old neighborhoods with high-rise slab, open space, high-rise slab, open space, high-rise slab, open space. . . . as far as the eye can see.

One of the hundreds of thousands of such Radiant City projects was a housing project called Pruitt-Igoe, built in the 1950s in St. Louis. It was designed by Minoru Yamasaki, a renowned architect, who later designed Manhattan's 100-story, twin-towered World Trade Center. It was highly praised at the time. The project consisted of 33 identical 11-story human filing cabinets, housing almost 3,000 families. One of the project's unusual features was an open corridor along the side of each slab, giving residents direct access to their apartments and some semiprivate open space. "Cheerful social enclaves," the architect called them. Another new feature was the "skip-stop" elevator, designed to save money by opening only at every third floor.

Yamasaki, like Le Corbusier, had hoped to use the open space between the high-rise slabs in creative ways. He wanted nice landscaping and buildings for recreation and community activities. Unlike Le Corbusier, he wanted to relieve the tedium of high-rises with a few low buildings. But this was a public housing project and the authorities were not inclined to waste money on such luxuries and frills for the poor.

Because St. Louis had special problems in assimilating the influx of southern blacks at the time, its industries fled to the outskirts. Pruitt-Igoe encountered racial tensions and rising black self-awareness. But these factors also prevailed elsewhere. There can be no question that architecture—the principles of *The Athens Charter*—were instrumental in causing the crime, alienation, and bitterness that pervaded the project—stench in the skip-stop elevators and the muggings in those galleries.

Over the years Pruitt-Igoe became irredeemably unlivable. In the end, there was nothing left for the authorities but to blow it up. The collapse—in a dynamite blast on April 21, 1972—of the first Pruitt-Igoe slab, seems to me to mark the beginning of the end of abstract architecture.

10 The Wrong State of Mind

"The problem of the house," Le Corbusier wrote more than half a century ago, "is a problem of the epoch. The stability of society depends on its solution."

Therefore, he declared, it is architecture's first duty to design housing for mass production, "to create the mass production spirit . . . the spirit of constructing mass production houses . . . the spirit of living in mass production houses . . . the spirit of conceiving mass production houses . . . the house-machine." As Le Corbusier saw it, the house-machine would be physically as well as morally healthy, and as beautiful as a good hand tool.

The only obstacle he saw was that "the right state of mind does not exist."

It still doesn't. Modern architecture has failed to kindle that spirit. On the contrary, the Modernists have helped squelch any public inclination to buy housing off the assembly line—not *modern* housing, at any rate.

Since the avant-garde set out to revolutionize building construction, we have all but completely mechanized farming, manufacturing, transportation, and communication. Construction remains the industry the industrial revolution has overlooked. Amid forests of office skyscrapers, maelstroms of freeways, and air-conditioned shopping malls, housing remains the problem of the epoch.

"It is by no means an overstatement to say that the housing

situation is the disgrace of American industry," *Fortune* magazine editorialized. The worst of the disgrace is that the editorializing was done in 1932.

Since then our ingenious species has invented television, electric carving knives, computerized dating services, and space travel to the moon and back. But *Fortune's* complaint that only half the homes of this country measure up to minimum standards of health and decency is still valid. Nearly half a century later it is still true, as the editorial said, that private enterprise "signally and magnificently muffed the opportunity to meet the needs of a huge potential market." It is still true that the building industry is not only poorly managed, but also disastrously dependent on speculative real estate dealers, costly methods, exorbitant rates of financing, obstructive tactics of labor, and the complications and stupidity of building codes and tax laws.

What is more, over half the country's families can no longer afford the "decent, safe, and sanitary housing in a suitable living environment" that Congress promised every American family in 1949. The chronic housing shortage persists, although there never seems to be a shortage of automobiles.

The Modernists tried. Le Corbusier labored for years, early in the 1920s, to get his Citrohan house mass-produced. His choice of name deliberately resembles Citroen, the French automobile, in hopes, I suppose, of production by association. But it did not work. Nor did Walter Gropius's "Series Houses," designed a few years later, which got no further than ecstatic Sunday supplement write-ups. The prototype models for several other modern prefabrications were approvingly pondered upon by middle-class intellectuals—and smirkingly rejected by the workers they were intended for.

Workers who spent all day with noisy machinery were in no mood to come home to a *machine à habiter* and drink beer in contortions of bent chrome pipes. They were not to be deprived of their bourgeois aspiration for doilies and overstuffed chairs. And without a mass market, there could be no mass production.

R. Buckminster Fuller, in 1929, charged that "the International Bauhaus," as he called it, lacked the proper comprehension of plumbing and other technologies. But his well-plumbed Dymaxion aluminum house was not put into production either. It only made a crowd-pulling display at Marshall Field department store in Chicago. A Dymaxion calf with two heads would have gotten the same attention.

Fuller went on to his Dymaxion bubble dome, which serves humanity at fairs and, in a small, portable version, in emergencies. It is shelter, not architecture.

In addition to Fuller's dome, other structural systems based on tensile strength, rather than compressive strength, have been developed over the past few decades. Luigi Nervi can make thin concrete shells stand up like folded paper to span large spaces. Konrad Wachsmann and others have engineered intricate space frames. Frey Otto designs huge, whimsically shaped tents that are supported by cables. Several temporary structures, used mainly for exhibition halls, consist of enormous balloons supported by air.

All of these new structural techniques create their own, often beautiful forms. All of them have been developed outside the Modern movement by engineers rather than architects, although architects at times apply the new techniques when large spans are required—for exhibit pavilions, sports arenas, auditoriums, or air terminals. So far, however, the new structures have not helped to bring "architecture back to earth and make a new home for man," as Lewis Mumford urged some time ago.

Instead, man and woman tried to do the best they could with what the "International Bauhaus" architects had given them.

An example is Pessac, near Bordeaux, designed by Le Corbusier in 1926. A project of 50 houses for the workers of a packing crate factory, it was commissioned by the factory owner, Henry Fruges, who asked his architect to make the houses pleasing to the people expected to live in them. Le Corbusier insisted on turning them into abstract compositions of open and enclosed Cubist forms, and painting them in

PESSAC BEFORE   PESSAC AFTER

primary colors. The art critics in Paris thought it was wonderful, but, for several years, the people of Pessac refused to move into what they called "the Moroccan village." Fruges got depressed.

A few years ago, Pessac was revisited by a French architect, Phillipe Boudon, who wrote a little book about it. He expected changes, but was not prepared, he reported, for the vengeance with which the residents went about turning the "living machines" into homes.

Some of the flat roofs are now pitched. The bright colors have disappeared. The wide ribbon windows have been narrowed. Patios have been enclosed. Open terraces have been roofed over. The spaces under the houses, which rest on stilts, have been walled in. Decorations have been fastened onto blank facades. Tool sheds and other structures add to general messiness. "In addition to the normal process of aging," Boudon observed, "there is also a real conflict between what the architect intended and what the occupants wanted."

This is a common experience in modern architecture. Where people cannot legally change their modern habitat, they fight it with vandalism.

There was no such conflict in the past. No one saw a need, for instance, to alter the facades John Wood designed some three hundred years ago in Bath, the lovely Georgian town in England. Two or more generations of residents seem entirely satisfied with the houses Clarence Stein and Henry Wright designed in a simple traditional style for Radburn, the new town in New Jersey, at about the same time Le Corbusier designed Pessac.

The hostility abstract architecture encounters almost everywhere is most recently illustrated by the fate of Paul Rudolph's famous Art and Architecture Building at Yale. The students so hated the building that it is assumed some of them were responsible for a damaging fire. The building is in gloomy disrepair—a slum.

This hostility is hardly conducive to the industrialization of housing production which, Le Corbusier and almost everyone tells us, is necessary if we are going to have decent housing in a suitable living environment for every family.

An effective building industrialization will require a new industry. Automobiles are not produced by carriage builders and stable masters. Xerox was not developed by carbon paper manufacturers. It is folly to assume that our antiquated, fragmented, and tradition-bound array of contractors, subcontractors, building trades, and building material manufacturers can pull themselves together to conceive, produce, and market new housing by new methods. Yet this is what architects, along with everyone else concerned, keep hoping.

At the end of World War II, attempts were made in this country to convert the aviation industry into housing production. The idea was to keep in service the factories that had suddenly stopped making bombers and fighter planes, by meeting the pent-up demand for decent shelter. Walter Gropius, Konrad Wachsmann, and others helped develop a prefabricated house.

Nothing came of it. The new product was hardly more alluring than Pessac, the Yale building, Pruitt-Igoe, or a quonset hut. Unwilling to set up their own distribution system, the prefabricators tried to market their houses through the established lumber dealers and building material suppliers. But the dealers could not be bothered, being much too busy getting rich on the suburban boom.

Next came George Romney from Detroit, the new Secretary of Housing and Urban Development, harboring high hopes for industrializing building techniques. In 1969, he launched

"Operation Breakthrough," a much-touted, national crusade to spread technology among the heathen in the sticks. It was a fiasco. The breakthrough broke down in local quibbles, red tape, and politics.

The lesson was that there is no point in mass-producing anything unless it can be shipped to the consumer easily and cheaply, either in one piece or in easily assembled components. To make the components fit, they must be standardized, which is difficult to do in a country where some 5,000 political jurisdictions have as many different ideas about what makes buildings safe—with as many written codes. Industrial production, furthermore, requires highly paid union labor, while most suburban home building is done by unorganized trades. Besides, even if you save 10, 20, or 30 percent of the construction cost, that is only a small amount of the total cost of a house. Construction, on the average, accounts for only 48 percent of the total. The rest is paid for land, the costs of borrowing money, sewers, and other utilities.

Sensible building industrialization, in brief, seems feasible only on a large scale—the scale of an entire new town of several thousand dwellings, built at once, with the component parts produced on site in a temporary factory, and put together assembly-line fashion.

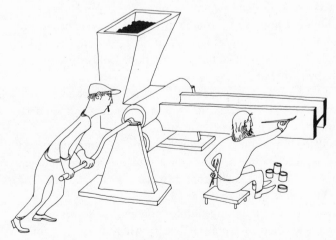

This is what Moshe Safdie had in mind when he designed his "Habitat '67" for the Montreal World's Fair. It is a hive of prefabricated concrete boxes stacked randomly in an open pyramid. The boxes form houses of different sizes with the roof of the house below serving as a garden terrace of the one above. The pyramid resembles a Mediterranean hilltown, with walkways, or "streets-in-the-sky" on different levels, providing a separate entrance to each house.

Safdie planned this "Habitat" for 1,000-2,000 houses and hoped to place a shopping center, a school, and other communal and commercial buildings in a park under the open pyramid. The Canadian government, however, did not want to risk such a large undertaking. It invested in the plant for casting the concrete boxes and installing the plumbing, wiring, insulation, and interior walls on the ground. It bought a three million dollar crane to lift the finished boxes into place. But then it used this equipment to build only 159 houses, which is not very many to pay off a heavy investment. Sure, everybody said. Habitat is nice, but too expensive. Safdie himself, although highly successful, cannot afford to live in his creation.

Most recently, Safdie designed a more advanced version of his modular, prefabricated housing for Coldspring, a new town within the city limits of Baltimore. Again, it seemed financially too risky to build the town all at once. When you build only a few hundred houses at a time, however, it is less expensive to build them in the laborious, traditional way than to set a complex industrial machinery in motion. Coldspring is now being built by hand.

We do have factory produced housing in this country. It is inexpensive. It is successful. It is depressing. And modern architecture has nothing to do with it.

In 1976, 11 million Americans lived in these "manufactured homes," alias "mobile homes," alias "trailers." Seven out of ten homes sold under $35,000 that year were mobile homes. The average mobile home cost was $11,000.

There is seldom anything mobile about mobile homes, except that they are hauled from the factory where they are built—

complete to the last built-in curtain rod and flower vase—to their site in a mobile home park. This once-in-a-lifetime trip accounts for the railroad car shape. In 43 states, the highway department will not permit anything wider than 14 feet to move down the road. (The remaining states permit 12 feet.)

The park site is usually rented for a nominal fee and once the mobile home is plugged into the water, sewer and electric lines, it is likely to stay put. If the owner moves, he or she will sell the home and perhaps buy another one in a different location. The late models therefore come without wheels, being moved on undercarriages that are taken back to the factory.

The fiction that mobile homes are mobile is carefully maintained, however, because it keeps costs down. The government taxes mobile homes as vehicles, rather than buildings. They are as easily financed as automobiles and, as a rule, not subject to the often expensive requirements of building and fire safety codes applied to stable structures. The result has often meant shoddy construction, hazards, and tragedies. Most mobile homes are manufactured by small companies that use cheap hardware, windows, cabinets and other furnishings, and pay low wages to an unsteady labor force. They are not constructed by advanced mass production techniques and don't make use of new technologies.

In 1976, however, Congress finally imposed federal minimum standards for the plumbing, heating and general safety of mobile homes, and the industry is now trying to change its image. The Mobile Home Manufacturers' Association has been renamed "Manufactured Housing Institute," and some models are beginning to conform to local building codes. They are also changing appearances, trying to look like buildings, rather than trailers, sporting pitched roofs, picture windows, terraces and fancy trim.

Manufactured or mobile, most established suburban communities consider mobile home parks no better than gypsy camps, and will not allow them. This means that only one of three mobile homes is located in a properly equipped park. The rest are scattered all over rural towns and country roads, adding nothing to the beauty of the countryside.

Some years ago, Vernon D. Swaback, an architect in Frank Lloyd Wright's former office at Taliesin, labored hard and intelligently to get the mobile industry interested in designs that would make their product more attractive and acceptable. He designed prototypes for handsomely landscaped parks with shrubbery and earth berms to make the mobile homes look stable. He suggested hinge-fold windows and walls that would not add to the width of the structure on the road, but could be pushed out upon arrival to make the trailer seem wider and more spacious.

The Frank Lloyd Wright-inspired models stole the show at several home builder convention exhibits, though they never went into producton. Nor did Paul Rudolph or other architects have any success in their attempts to use mobile homes—with their cost advantages—as building blocks for larger, more livable structures. Efforts to combine mobile homes into something better went no further than stacking two trailers atop each other to make two-story models. The manufactured home industry, in short, has been no more able or willing to improve itself or its product than the conventional home building industry.

But perhaps we should stop deploring the lack of progress in building technology and find solace in the fact that a house is not a machine. For all the inefficiences, high cost, and other failings, we should be grateful that our shelter is still built by human hands requiring human skill.

Besides, what compels us to go on mechanizing and automating people out of satisfying work, and out of the satisfactions of craftsmanship and personal accomplishment? Our cities, to say nothing of the cities in developing countries, are swollen with people who came from farms—without education or industrial skills—looking for work that is not there. They would be well employed in the building and rebuilding of a more human environment.

11 Downfall of the High-Rise

Almost 40 years after *The Athens Charter* was drafted, another boatload of architects, urbanists, and scientists cruised through the Mediterranean in search of an urban vision.

There were ten such annual conference cruises, with some 40 or 50 participants each. Their host was the Greek city planner Constantinos Doxiadis. Among the regular guests were economist Barbara Ward, anthropologist Margaret Mead, designer-philosopher Buckminster Fuller, historian Arnold Toynbee, sociologist Marshall McLuhan, architect-planner Lord Richard Llewelyn-Davies, biologist Jonas Salk, and geographer-urbanist Jean Gottman. Doxiadis's purpose was to bring a variety of expertise to bear on urban problems, and to develop what he called *"Ekistiks,* the science of human settlements." After five days of cruising, talking *Ekistiks,* and exploring Greek islands, each group met for a ceremonial session in the amphitheater of Delos and, by the light of torches held by sailors, signed a joint declaration. In effect, although not by conscious intent, the Declarations of Delos try to undo CIAM.

The last of these declarations, Delos Ten, condemns high-rise and large-scale buildings. "They should not," it says, "be considered as the normal, general, and most suitable method of expanding and renewing our cities." Doxiadis himself put it more strongly. In the tradition of architectural criminality, no doubt, he startled his guests at one of the shipboard sessions with what he called a confession of his "crimes—crimes against the city. My greatest crime," he said, "was the construction of high-rise buildings."

Doxiadis spoke like a war college officer lecturing on the perfect cavalry charge, drawing arrows and circles on a blackboard, and explaining things by numbers. Here is the thrust of his charge:

One: The great cities of the past keep people and buildings in balance with nature, but high-rise buildings work against nature. They destroy the scale of the landscape and obstruct normal air circulation, causing poisonous pockets of automobile and industrial pollution to collect.

Two: High-rise buildings work against man himself because

they isolate him, and his isolation is an important factor in the rising crime rate. Children suffer most because they lose direct, spontaneous contacts with nature and other children. They can leave the confinement of their apartments only under parental control. This restricts the parents as well as the children.

Three: High-rise buildings work against society because they prevent the basic social units—the family, the extended family, and the neighborhood—from functioning naturally.

Four: High-rise buildings work against the network of transportation, communication, and utilities, because they overload it or, in any event, distribute the load unevenly. High-rises lead to congested roads, and wasteful maldistribution of water, electric power, and sewers.

Five: High-rise buildings destroy the urban landscape by dwarfing traditional human symbols such as churches, mosques, temples, city halls, and other buildings that traditionally towered over the city.

"We may not agree that God or government should rise above people," Doxiadis said "but are we ready to agree that symbols of capital gain should rise above everything else?" Does it make sense that we obliterate historic villages and towns with high-rise hotels built for visitors who come to enjoy the charm?

It obviously doesn't, and it is evident that Doxiadis expressed what many people have long felt. Similar charges have been heard for years in countless suburban zoning hearings: High-rises block our views, they cause traffic congestion, they attract "undesirable" people, or too many newcomers, they lower property values, they interfere with television reception, they cause gusts of wind, they consume more than their share of energy, and produce more than their share of waste and pollution. Far from representing "progress," as too many businessmen and politicians still assume, high-rise buildings can ruin their neighborhood and depress downtown business districts. San Francisco architect Beverly Willis calls them "coffins in the sky."

In San Francisco, where a 60-foot height limitation was put

to a referendum in the 1972 election, high-rise opponents pointed out that the city budget had gone up 39 percent between 1963 and 1972 when 33 high-rise apartments were built. The city's crime increased by 119 percent and commuter traffic by 50 percent. San Francisco's population, however, went down by 15 percent. The referendum failed. But the civic sentiment it revealed caused city planners to limit the building height to 160 feet in San Francisco's central business district, and to 40 feet in the rest of the city.

In Washington, D.C., at about the same time, local business leaders were once again agitating for tall buildings. Washington's height limitation was imposed by Congress in 1910, to make sure that no building should be taller than the Capitol. As a general rule (with some complicated exceptions) the law permits buildings to be as high as the width of the street or avenue on which they are located, plus 20 feet. This gives the capital a pleasant distinction. Thomas Jefferson wanted "the houses low & convenient & the streets light & airy."

There was to be a hearing before the D.C. Zoning Commission on the matter, and I was preparing to testify—composing gushing prose about how increased building heights would raise the tide of parking lots, the waves of crime and iniquity, the number of unemployed, the bankruptcy of small businessmen and the exodus of taxpayers—when a friend called to say that Nathaniel Alexander Owings, *the* Owings of Skidmore, Owings and Merrill, would also testify on the morrow.

Damn.

Skidmore, Owings and Merrill has designed more and higher skyscrapers than any other firm of architects. It gave us the 1,107-foot-high John Hancock Center and the 1,450-foot-high Sears Building in Chicago, just to top New York's World Trade Center by 100 feet.

I could just see it. I had seen it many times. These skyscraping masterbuilders always come on with a bodyguard of handsome young architects, armed with neatly indexed ring binders full of phony statistics, at least two slide projectors, and one high fidelity tape recorder. They flash double barrages of breathtaking color photographs—the sun setting on a global array of glass towers, interspersed with mind-boggling charts of corporate cash, flowing straight into municipal treasuries—all of this to the accompaniment of Haydn's Horn Concerto with voiced over quotations from Michelangelo and Santayana.

I preceded Nat Owings at the hearing with the thought that Michelangelo, Santayana and Owings would have the last word.

Nat Owings appeared alone, just his beaming, jovial, slightly rotund self. He began with a joyous jingle (flattering references to the dignity of the capital and the wisdom of the commissioners assembled), but soon worked himself up to sound like the bells of St. Peter's.

"History has proven," he intoned, "that skyscrapers tend to dehumanize the area in which they are raised. They suck the lifeblood of the area around them, drawing into the air what should be closer to the human scale." He continued with an earnestly persuasive tolling of arguments to hold the capital's height just where it is.

Since then, the boys in the back room have, for the time being, lowered their visions of high-rising profits—in Washington, that is.

Owings was right about history. Citizen complaints against tall buildings were voiced as long ago as the second century A.D. by the Roman satirist Juvenal. He railed against the proliferation of high-rise apartments in Rome, some of which rose 100 feet above the sidewalk. According to Juvenal, most of them were held up with props, and their huge cracks were merely plastered over by the landlords. Like so many skyscrapers today, they were towering infernos. Roof tiles kept falling from lofty heights. Vases were knocked out of upper story windows, and chamber pots were emptied on the street, too frequently on the heads of passing citizens. Crime was so rampant within and around Rome's high-rise slums that people made their wills before venturing out of their apartments.

Nineteen hundred years later, high-rise apartment houses are

hardly safer. Architect Oscar Newman, in a study conducted at
New York University (which he later elaborated for the
National Institute of Law Enforcement and Criminal Justice),
reported that the crime rate in low-income housing projects
around the country increases in proportion to building height.

The total number of crimes of all kinds, Newman found, is
three times higher in towering elevator apartment buildings
than in neighborhoods of detached houses, townhouses and
walk-up apartments inhabited by people of the same social and
economic group.

Newman's explanation is persuasive: In a high-rise apartment house corridor, the only "defensible space," as he calls it,
is the apartment itself. Everything else is a "no man's land," that
is neither public or private. Unlike streets—which are watched
by old folks looking out of the window, shopkeepers,
bartenders, policemen, somebody—high-rise corridors and
lobbies are sparsely used. Neighbors rarely know each other
and have no way of telling a resident from a stranger who may
be up to no good. Victims are trapped in corridors and
elevators, while criminals can easily escape down different fire
stairs or across the roof.

In walk-up buildings, where only a few families share the
same entrance, people know each other and quickly detect
suspicious intruders. The hallways and staircases become
extensions of the home—neighbors sit on the chairs and stoops
and chat, they store bicycles and other items there, they sweep
up. The street, too, becomes part of the shared and protected
neighborhood territory.

"Kids can play outside and still be within calling distance of
the window. And as parents supervise their children at play,
they also monitor street life. Defensible space is extended. You
begin to get safe streets as well as safe buildings," wrote
Newman.

There is something sadly amiss when going out to play is not
a matter of a friendly parental shove out the back door, but
requires a major expedition down the hall, into the elevator,

across the lobby, and, more often than not, across dangerous parking lots and a street with heavy traffic—an expedition that usually requires proper timing and scheduling because it involves a parental escort, at least until the child is tall enough to reach the elevator button. The parent complicates things because he or she will want to combine the expedition with some other errand.

And there the parent sits on the playground bench, pretending to read a book, but reading mostly the face of the child to see if it shows signs of tiring. Or reading the watch to see if the allotted time is up. Or reading the sky to see if perchance some rain might come to the rescue. Watching a child on a public playground is not the same as playing with him in a garden or in the fields.

The Department of Housing and Urban Development now officially counsels against building high-rise, low-income housing projects.

Great Britain's National Society for the Prevention of Cruelty to Children called high-rise apartments "restrictive, undesirable and productive, in sum, of a good deal of human suffering." They are now banned in London.

The rich can buy defenses against crime. Luxury high-rise apartments have around-the-clock guards, doormen and electronic monitoring equipment. But even in the high-rent districts there is more crime in tall elevator buildings than in townhouses. An entrance that is shared by too many people who do not know one another invites trouble. This may be one reason that high-rise luxury apartment construction dropped 78 percent between 1972 and 1976.

The conventional justification for high-rise apartments is that they are less expensive to build and to maintain, and that they accommodate higher densities than low buildings. Neither is correct.

As Newman explains, the assertion that high-rises are less expensive than walk-ups is a confusion between the overall "development costs" of a housing development and its "construction costs," and between the maintenance costs of buildings occupied by different family types. Development costs include the cost of the land; construction costs are exclusive of land costs. The higher the cost of a piece of land, the less will be the development cost per unit if more units can be put on the same piece of land. A fair comparison can therefore be made only if both the high-rise and the low-rise have comparable densities. Studies by the Department of Housing and Urban Development show that under a fair comparison, the development cost of a four-family walk-up apartment is usually about half as much per room as the cost of a room in a high-rise apartment that requires expensive foundations, elevators and other mechnical equipment. The construction cost of a walk-up is about one-third of an average high-rise.

Nor is it essential to build high to achieve high densities. High densities are often frowned on because they are confused with crowding, which is like confusing an Easter parade with a riot. In other words, the presence of relatively large numbers of people on a relatively small number of square feet is not necessarily bad. It depends on how the people and the space are organized. With proper organization, high densities are very desirable. It is desirable for people who choose to live close to their work, near cultural attractions or public transportation stops, or to share an exceptional view.

People living close together also tend to require less energy— they are huddled together for warmth, as it were. For all their sealed, air-conditioned, brightly-lit buildings, traffic jams, and screeching subway trains, New York City consumes about half the energy per resident as the rest of the country. The entire New York urban region, with its 9.7 percent of the nation's population, earning 12 percent of the nation's money income, consumes only 6.4 percent of the nation's energy, according to the New York Regional Planning Association.

The reason clever architects can house as many people close to the ground as up in the sky is that skyscrapers have to be spaced widely apart to admit sunlight into their groundfloor apartments. This space can be used to house people in various ways—in narrow single family townhouses with patios; or, two duplex apartments, one with a patio and the other with a terrace. A recent housing project of this kind in the Bronx accommodated as many families per acre as the four 20-story apartment houses permitted in the same amount of land. The cost was about the same. Living conditions are incomparably better—particularly for the children who run out of the house to play.

12 The Skyline

High-rise office buildings are no more efficient than high-rise apartment buildings. But office enterprises continue their fondness for skyscrapers. I suspect this is not because waiting for an elevator is more efficient than walking down the hall, but because it is not inefficient enough to outweigh the skyscraper's value as an advertisement. Corporations and developers sacrifice efficiency for prestige, much as the noble families of medieval San Gimignano sacrificed convenience for the pleaure of building higher towers than their rivals. Other Italian citizens of the time would have none of this. They did not permit tall buildings to interfere with winter sun and summer breezes, and prohibited any buildings higher than the municipal tower, let alone the cathedral.

Modern cities are only beginning to see the folly of high-rising vanity. Tall buildings do not save land or make money for anyone, except possibly their owners. They are fearfully expensive for the community, the reason being that, as long as we can't stack automobiles on top of one another as cheaply as we can stack people, we are not saving any space at all. And since most people, unfortunately, come in automobiles, the land saved by building vertically rather than horizontally, is wasted on moving and parking the additional cars. Any higher tax revenues that may result from higher concentrations are usually spent on the additional services needed.

The setback and small parks that may be gained on the ground are dubious gains. They are drafty. Wind hits the top of the skyscraper and builds such pressure as it blows down the building facade that it is a gale by the time it bounces off the street. Engineers call this the "Monroe effect," named for the winds that teased Marilyn Monroe's skirt in *The Seven Year Itch*. The plaza of the Boston Prudential Center had to be enclosed so people would not be blown into the fountain. Wind pressure shattered most of the first glass panes of the rivaling Hancock Tower down the street. Even 10- or 15-story buildings can make the "microclimate" around them unpleasant.

High-rises can also be fire hazards. They are difficult to evacuate. Fire experts will tell you that the danger of fire grows with the number of occupants and the size of a building. Safety precautions become more complex because ladders and water pressure go only so high. If the building is sealed, heat and smoke are sucked up elevator shafts and fire stairs and cannot escape. Breaking windows to let the smoke escape can kill people down on the street.

It is impossible to evacuate people in a short time. Fire fighting in a skyscraper is complex and dangerous. The fire risks are greater in residential skyscrapers because the pipes are concealed and it is difficult to inspect the sprinkler system regularly. Some builders do not even install them, because they add about 4 percent to the construction cost.

Yet most cities have succumbed. In Paris, some years ago, President Georges Pompidou permitted exceptions to the traditional 102-feet height limit. Now the enchanting Ile St. Louis-Notre Dame-Pantheon skyline is disfigured with a 23-story glass and aluminum box perched atop the Halle-aux-Vine. The clumsy high-rise cluster at La Defense mars the view beyond the Arc de Triomphe. There is a 50-story, 689-foot tower on the site of the old Montparnasse railroad station.

But the greatest shame is what happened to Jerusalem.

In the flush of Israel's 1967 victory, Jerusalem decided to embrace progress, American style, with housing projects and towering hotels. Some Israeli planners disagreed with Mayor Teddy Kollek's skyscraper and freeway ambitions. To prove them wrong, the mayor invited a number of internationally famous architects, urbanists and artists, including America's Buckminster Fuller, Louis Kahn, and Philip Johnson, to endorse his ambitions. His Honor was quite surprised when his guests expressed their "unqualified" condemnation. Louis Kahn deplored the invasion of "money buildings." Buckminster Fuller denounced "the high-rise wall of greed."

More effective than these condemnations was a proposal to build a 24-story Hyatt House Hotel on top of Mount Scopus. That shocked the city into adopting a height limitation. I wish it had come in time. It didn't. Far too much damage had been done to Jerusalem in four or five misguided years.

In America's great cities, notably in New York and Chicago, the skyscraper is at home. Manhattan and the Loop are among the most American of America's historic expressions and accomplishments, symbols of the country's energy and power. They deserve all the sonnets written to them. They are modern San Gimignanos, or even cathedrals. They have no rivals in their own time.

And there is romance living in these glass towers. Deep silencing shadows creep across the bustling canyons below. Slowly the lights turn on across the skyline. They twinkle hesitantly in the dusk, as the ice tinkles in the martini glass. A tugboat—there has got to be a tugboat—sighs its way down . . . what? The East River? Lake Michigan? The San Francisco Bay?

And yet this Promethean vanity is now as outdated as Wagnerian castles on the Rhine. It does not diminish their awesome beauty to say that corporate high-rise palaces no longer express our concepts of livability. The Reformation has not diminished the grandeur of Chartres.

Lately, architects are demeaning the spirit of these great skylines: Manhattan with the domineering World Trade Center; Chicago with Hancock and Sears; Boston with Hancock and Prudential; San Francisco with Transamerica; Seattle with Commerce House. All these buildings, I fear, are but silly stunts. As happened with other styles and building types, greatness degenerated into mannerist exhibitionism. After the acrobats come the clowns.

There is no further need for high-rise buildings. They should certainly no longer "be considered the normal, general, and most suitable method of expanding and renewing our cities."

America's great historic skylines should be declared national monuments to be carefully preserved, thoughtfully changed and improved, if necessary, but not expanded. All construction should be controlled to preserve the skyline's aesthetic integrity. But more important than the distant view and the grand towers are the spaces in between, the spaces that must be made fit for people to talk, sit, shop, get around, and look around with ease and pleasure.

13 Las Vegas Is Not Almost All Right

In the first three-quarters of this century, life in the industrialized world has changed more radically than in any equivalent time span. Yet, like abstract art, abstract architecture has remained strangely static.

A 1924 propeller airplane, for instance, strikes us as amusingly antiquated today. Most people, however, still find Marcel Breuer's tubular steel chair, or a Mondrian painting of 50 years ago uncomfortably novel. And newly created—or imitated—metal furniture of a different bent, or garish geometric patterns on large canvases are still touted as new and original, dazzling the "with-it" art crowd and inspiring ponderous reviews.

The same is true of architecture. There is nothing on the photographs of early modern classics by Mies van der Rohe, Eric Mendelsohn, or Le Corbusier to suggest that they were built half a century and more ago, except, perhaps, the old-fashioned automobiles parked in front of the buildings, and the clothing of people who stand in the picture.

The grand, old avant-garde of the architectural revolution died off in the 1960s and '70s. The second and third generations of Modernists who took its place are fervently stomping the same ground, marking time. Variations between early and late modern seem superficial and personal. This is not to say that there is not, occasionally, some good work by a dozen or so good artists.

Until his change of heart and mind, Philip Johnson varied the Miesian tradition only by adorning the glass box with touches of historicism or absurd shapes. The change came suddenly in the spring of 1978, surprising everyone and infuriating some: Johnson presented the model of a Manhattan skyscraper, designed for AT&T, that continued where McKim, Mead & White had left off at the turn of the century and ended in a dramatic finial, shaped like a "Chippendale" broken pediment. (Minoru Yamasaki and Edward Durell Stone had trifled with the Miesian box merely by giftwrapping it in grilles, flutes, and tinsel.)

Ieoh Min Pei also stayed essentially with Mies, but cut the cubes into triangles with razor-sharp edges that cut all pretense of functionalism into very precise shreds. This nevertheless yielded a superb work of architecture—the East Building of the National Gallery of Art in Washington, D.C., rivaling Eero Saarinen's Dulles Airport Terminal as the most inspired building of our time.

Eero Saarinen, who died in 1961 at the age of 51, designed forceful, spirited, and flowing new building forms, such as Eric Mendelsohn had envisioned more than 40 years earlier in tiny sketches he made in the trenches of World War I. Saarinen's partner and successor, Kevin Roche, is less baroque but similarly inventive. Harry Weese designs refreshingly simple and handsome buildings.

Paul Rudolph attained fleeting stardom with a Le Corbusier stunt—the Art and Architecture Building at Yale. It is one of the disasters of contemporary architecture, as I mentioned earlier. The only architect who can successfully apply Le Corbusier's style is José Luis Sert. He is, in my view, a better architect than Le Corbusier, because his architecture is rational.

Marcel Breuer and Gordon Bunshaft, who began in the Miesian tradition, also turned to Le Corbusier sculptures, making up with pharaonic heaviness what they lack in agility. There is an awful lot of concrete around—some bending backwards, like Bunshaft's hideous ski-jump-shaped skycraper in Manhattan, some modeled into nicely balanced Cubist compositions, like Kallman, McKinnel and Knowles' handsome city hall in Boston.

This proclivity for heavy concrete—often called "brutalist"—seems anachronistic. Technology is striving these days to make things lighter, with light-weight metals, tensile structures, air pressure-supported balloon domes, and electronic miniaturization. Why, then, does architecture persist in weighty monumentality and mausoleam permanence?

There was only one notable newcomer to mid-century architecture. Louis Kahn had not advanced with the Modern movement. He suddenly emerged from relative obscurity with the Richards Medical Research Building at Philadelphia. It is a building without modern precedent, relying almost entirely on Kahn's artistic intuition for arranging brick arches and San Gimignano towers in formal patterns. He talked more than he built, and talked in mystical abstractions; he was therefore widely idolized as architecture's messiah. Kahn's style, however, is too personal to be successfully adopted and adapted by others.

And that's about it. The rest of them seem more intent on creating attention than architecture. You get attention, at least in the architectural magazines, by letting it all hang out, as it were—likely and unlikely ducts, railings, metal trellises, unexplained pipes, exposed beams, inexplicable tubes, and innards in raw colors that would brighten the boiler room of a mothballed destroyer, but do little for the lobby of a concert hall.

Or you might get attention—a page in the *New York Times* Sunday magazine—by nailing a heavy molding all around the midriff of a humdrum stucco house, or hiding the house behind a false facade with a round hole cut into the front. The architects of these experiments call themselves "post-Modernists" and are also known as "cardboard Corbusiers."

Most noted architects, Miesian or Corbusian, think of themselves as avant-garde. *Avant* of what? As I said earlier, there are no troops behind them. The younger members of the profession seem to be drifting off into different directions, fads, and fashions. Sigfried Giedion deplored this trend towards what he called "playboy architecture."

The trouble is that the boys don't have much to play with unless they get a very special commission—a piece of what Paul Rudolph has called "foreground architecture." The background—the apartment houses, offices, and stores that determine the looks of our place to live—is mostly decided by zoning commissioners, who ordain a building's shape and height; by building coders, who prescribe most of what can or cannot be done; by mortgage bankers, who decide whether to invest in cheap or quality materials and construction; and by engineers, who more or less design the structure to meet all these specifications. This leaves the architect to wrap a pretty package and decorate it with a shiny bauble of a lobby. The building is styled—styled in the latest architectural fashion. Grilles are out. Ski jumps are in. So are ten-story, glass-roofed atrium courts full of live vegetables. Perhaps Pierre Cardin or Halston ought to enter the exterior decorating business. They might introduce something fresh.

Something fresh is needed, because the Modernists have been so insistent on changing our life that they have done little to enhance life as it is.

Admittedly, it is not easy to enhance life without changing the system. Le Corbusier proposed to put buildings on stilts, so people could walk under them. He also proposed putting playgrounds on the roof to return the space the building takes. But the ideas were not fresh enough to change the greed of developers who put buildings on stilts, all right, but then enclosed the space and rented it. Only a few builders care about roof gardens enough to grapple with building and fire codes, additional elevators and staircases, and higher assessments.

Only a strong public demand could compel the extra investment and cooperation of authorities. But an understandably wary public demands only that Le Corbusier high-rises not be built—at least, "not in my front yard."

In sum, the Modern movement could not keep what it promised. It brought us some interesting and even some beautiful buildings—a few rare masterpieces for esoteric enjoyment. But people have gained little from the architectural revolution. More often than not, its products are aesthetically disruptive, functionally deficient, and urbanistically wrong.

The new technical conveniences, such as elevators or air-conditioning, are just as convenient when they are installed in Victorian or neoclassic buildings. Our modern museums, opera houses, or city halls often function quite well. But they function no better, even in terms of twentieth-century style and technology, than museums, opera houses, or city halls built in other times.

Would-be masterbuilders of the "total man-made environment" actually design very little of it. I am not sure whether that is good or bad.

Probably only 5 percent of what is being built in this country is designed by our roughly 50,000 registered architects. Half of them, according to 1976 statistics, are members of the American Institute of Architects, which imposes ethical and professional rules of conduct. In 1977, fewer than 4 percent of all AIA members were women. Fewer than 1 percent were black. The majority of architects worked in small firms of fewer than 20 employees, while a handful of large firms, such as Skidmore, Owings and Merrill (employing over 800 people in five branch offices), designed virtually all the dominant corporation palaces.

Most heavy construction work is not designed but engineered. Engineers in this country do not, as a rule, have much flair for aesthetics.

Only on rare occasions will an architect be invited to design a power dam or highway bridge. It was something of a miracle that architect Harry Weese was appointed as an equal of engineers to design the new subway system for Washington, D.C. It turned out beautifully.

Practically all residential buildings are designed by builders and land developers without benefit of architect. The overwhelming majority of our subdivision homes, townhouses, and apartment buildings consist of a basic structure that will meet the minimum standards set by the building codes. Minimum standards turn out to be maximum standards, for why should a builder invest more than he must? The skeleton is then enclosed with wall panels, floors, and roofing, and equipped with doors, windows, mechanical equipment, and hardware selected from the latest annual edition of *Sweet's*, the voluminous catalog listing thousands of different building products made in this country. Variations in styling or exterior decoration can turn the same basic structure into a Cinderella-colonial or split-level Regency.

The guiding principle of this assembly is to achieve what the builder considers to be the greatest possible sales appeal. The customers' chief concern is the amount of space and convenience of location they get for their money. With its emphasis on ample plumbing, new housing in America reflects our high standard of living. It is not matched by an equally high level of taste, nor what I would call a sense of livability. The consumer movement has not yet reached the consumers of architecture and urban design.

Ralph Nader has improved automobile safety. Adelle Davis and others who have spoken and written about food have, without doubt, improved nutrition in this country and made people aware of the ill effects of edible junk. There has been no similarly sustained effort to inform and educate the public about the effect of junk building and urban design on their lives.

Our newspapers have book critics, art critics, movie critics, television critics, fashion and garden editors. But there are only three or four full-time architecture critics writing for American newspapers. A few more are allowed to tuck an occasional piece on the built world into the real estate section or the arts page. Magazines that deal with our place to live are mainly interested in sofas and potted plants. Nothing worthy of discussion seems to have been built in America's television land since the tube's only art and architecture commentator, Aline Saarinen, died some years ago.

The few architecture critics around have, like art critics, defended abstract modernism and ignored the fact that the majority of people ignored it. Important exceptions are Lewis Mumford and Jane Jacobs. Mumford, in his "Skyline" column in *The New Yorker*, pointed out the follies of Le Corbusier almost as soon as they were committed. Jane Jacobs wrote that superb book, *The Death and Life of Great American Cities*, which, more than anything else, helped to stop the urban renewal bulldozers.

The rest of us had grown up with the Modern movement. Its leaders were our friends. Our love for art and architecture was a love for modern art and architecture. Our concern for bettering our surroundings meant to make our surroundings more modern. This is not to say that I ever thought everything modern was good. I have for years made my living criticizing the faults I find in contemporary design and extolling forgotten virtues of the past. And yet, the basic credo of modernism was also my own article of faith, the standards of my judgments. All of us who are writing on architecture built our reputations on that faith. It is not easy to restructure.

However, it is easier for a writer on architecture to—shall we say?—expand his critical faculties, than it is for an art critic or curator. By praising an artist or style, they invest not only their own reputations, but also the reputations and fortunes—often vast amounts of money—of museums, collectors, and dealers. It is difficult for a museum curator to tell his trustees: "I changed my mind about that forceful spatial integrity of Helen Franckenthaler. It's really a put on. Sorry I got you to spend $250,000 for that thing."

If critics said nothing, architects said less. Architecture

students might grumble that "less is a bore," and Edward Durell Stone announced early in the sixties that he would "go to bat for beauty." But only Robert Venturi, joined later by his wife, Denise Scott Brown, challenged the basic tenets of modernism.

Venturi's first critique of the terrible oversimplifications of modernism, its pious purism, antihistoricism, and, as Vincent Scully called it, "spinsterish disdain for the popular culture," was published in 1966 under the auspices of the Museum of Modern Art in New York. He entitled the book *Complexity and Contradiction in Architecture,* favoring both. He says, rightly, that they are the stuff of which cities are made. The book deals mainly with aesthetics. As to modernism, Venturi states his "intense admiration of its early period, when its founders, sensitive to their own times, proclaimed the right revolution. Our argument lies mainly with the irrelevant and distorted prolongation of that old revolution today."

From complexities and contradictions in historic buildings and cities, Venturi advanced—to Las Vegas. In its terrifying pop vulgarity, he sought the inspiration architects of old had found in the temples of antiquity, and that which the modern avant-garde had found in American grain elevators. Mesmerized by the messiness of Route 91, "the archetype of the commercial strip," Venturi proclaimed the Las Vegas billboards "almost all right." He and his students measured the distance between each wantonly hurled-down filling station and neon-flashing super-sign, much as archeologists measure classic column spacing.

"The archetypal Los Angeles," he concluded, "will be our Rome, and Las Vegas our Florence; and like the archetypal grain elevators some generations ago, the Flamingo sign will be the model to shock our sensibilities towards a new architecture."

It will, I trust, do no such thing. Look where those grain elevators got us.

Venturi's horrifying idea is based on several misunderstandings. In the first place, neither Los Angeles nor the Las Vegas strip happened for or on behalf of people. They happened for automobiles and the scale and speed of automobility. They are a chaotic Ville Radieuse. Is that not what we are fighting?

Surely there is excitement, a sensuous and romantic

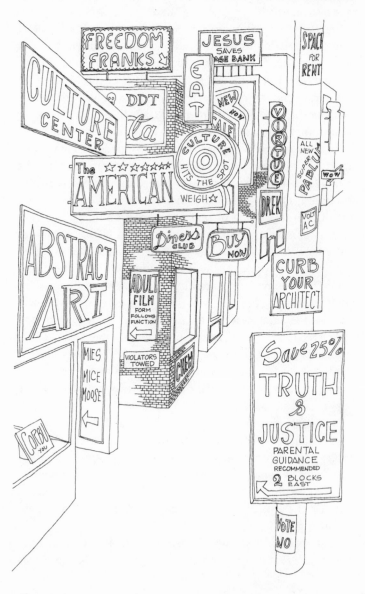

excitement, on the strip, in contrast to the Miltown boredom of modern developments. Las Vegas is a fun place to gamble, but not many Americans would want to live there—at least not near the strip. Most of us resent billboards, high-rises and other "commercial intrusions" in our neighborhoods.

The worst misunderstanding is the assertion that the strip and its neon screams are spontaneous expressions of the American soul, the apogee of American folk art. Rubbish! Most of the billboards and all of the gas stations were contrived by ad agency designers, not to represent the taste of people, but to titillate their appetites, to sell them things they often don't want. To sell, sell, sell. One might call the ambiguous kitsch and nefarious gobbledygook of America's greedy, corporate hucksterism the opiate of the people.

Pop art, in short, is not popular art. It is a sometimes witty but highly intellectual irony. Robert Indiana's ubiquitous "LOVE" sign aside, how many Jasper Johns or Roy Lichtenstein reproductions do you see on the walls of American middle-class homes?

No, thank you, we do not need more pop architecture. The golden arches and cutesy colonial roadside stands suffice.

Venturi is right that a new architecture must spring from the vernacular, that it must reconnect with instinctive wisdom. Denise Scott Brown is right that, "architects must learn to respect other people's values." These values, however, are not represented by the Flamingo sign, but by the New England commons and the southwestern mission church; not by the grain elevator, but by the barn.

The strip leads only to further chaos and alienation and violence. We yearn for order, community, and yes, love, in our place to live.

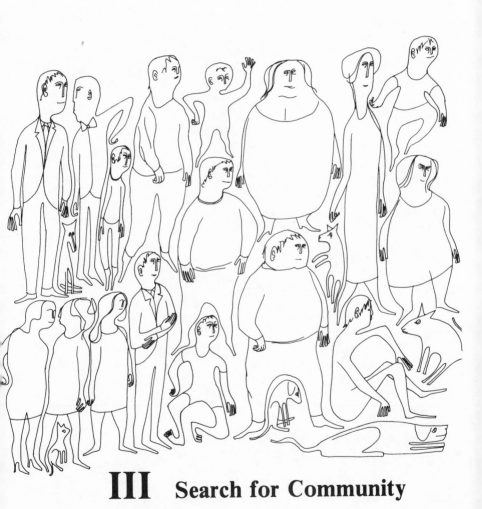

III Search for Community

14 A Peaceful Path to Real Reform

George Bernard Shaw called Sir Ebenezer Howard "the mildest and most unassuming of men . . . . an elderly nobody . . . . whom the Stock Exchange would have dismissed as a negligible crank."

He wore a droopy walrus mustache, dressed in a shabbily conventional way, and made his living as a stenographer. He was devoted to Esperanto. He spent much time tinkering with his inventions, among them improvements of the Remington typewriter and a shorthand machine. His most important invention was a practical system of what he called "social cities" to assure orderly urban growth.

Shaw said that he was "one of those heroic simpletons who do big things whilst our prominent worldlings are explaining why they are utopian and impossible."

Prominent worldlings, particularly in America, are still at it, oblivious to the fact that Howard's concept has been successfully realized in Great Britain and that it serves as the basis for urban planning in most of the world. (Only in America is planning for orderly urban growth still underdeveloped. We dabble at best in sporadic city planning.)

The Modern movement embraced Howard's formula of building complete new communities as satellites of the old central cities, rather than letting the cities spread indiscriminately and destructively like cancer. But it negated the spirit of Howard's scheme.

Le Corbusier called the city "man's grip on nature." It is a total, totalitarian grip of steel, concrete, and macadam. Howard originally called his new communities "garden cities." He would build them not to grip nature, but to harmonize with nature.

Howard extolls this harmony and the bounty of Mother Nature's bosom with Victorian exuberance. But the sentimentality contains a presentiment of the perceptive urban planning theories of Sir Patrick Geddes.

Geddes, a Scottish biologist, sociologist, and urban planner, and a contemporary of Howard's, was the first, in Lewis Mumford's words, "to understand the organic interdependence of city and region as the basic geographic and historic structure underlying the complex interaction of place, work, people, and of educational, aesthetic, and political activities." He was the first to recognize the urban ecology and the imperative of matching it to the natural ecology.

Geddes's planning theories, although at first sensed rather than articulated by Howard and his friends, became the premise of Howard's "town and country planning" movement. It stands, in Mumford's phrase, for "organic planning," and thus, for precisely the opposite of the technocratic planning and authoritarian formalism of the Modernists.

Le Corbusier and the Bauhaus set out to solve the same city problems that Howard tried to solve—the crowding, anonymity, and blight brought about by mechanized industry. They saw the solution in more mechanization, in turning not just the house, but the entire city into "a machine for living." The result was almost all machine and no living.

Howard, being preoccupied with practical-social rather than abstract-aesthetic questions, and not being addled by idolatry of the machine, was concerned with livability. His solution was to humanize and decentralize the city. He anticipated the philosophy that economist E.F. Schumacher outlined 75 years later in his book, *Small Is Beautiful*.

Ebenezer Howard was born in 1850 in London. His father was a baker who started work at 3 a.m. and kept at it well into the evening. His mother worked in the bakery. Only four of their nine children survived infancy.

Young Ebenezer went to school at the age of four and traveled to America at the age of 21. He tried farming in Iowa but failed. He moved on to Chicago, grateful that he had taught himself Pitman's shorthand, which proved more lucrative.

His preoccupation at the time seems to have been religion. In any event, he later denied having had any particular interest in city planning while he was in Chicago. Some of his biographers believe, nevertheless, that he must have visited Riverside, a carefully planned suburban community that was then being built four miles beyond the city limits.

Riverside's designer was Frederick Law Olmsted, the landscape architect who had become famous with his design for New York's Central Park. At Riverside, as at Berkeley, he and his partner, architect Calvert Vaux, applied some of the same principles of designing with nature, rather than putting it in man's grip. In contrast to the gridiron pattern that prevails in most American towns and cities, the roads meander with the lay of the land. Vehicles and people are separated on roads and walkways. Care is taken to preserve the natural topography and ecology, to save not only the cost of later landscaping, but, as Olmsted put it, "to imply leisure, contemplativeness and happy tranquility." Small parks and ample playgrounds complete this tableau.

Olmsted told the developers of Riverside that while he was aiming for a distinctly rural and open atmosphere, "in those special features whereby the town is distinguished from the country, there should be the greatest possible contrast which is compatible with the convenient communication and pleasant abode of a community." The shopping center was to be urban in character. In short, Olmsted's Riverside, designed in 1869, aimed at the "marriage between town and country" that Howard advocated two decades later. It is difficult to believe that there is not at least a subliminal connection.

It is also beside the point. Howard never claimed to have invented "garden cities" or "new towns," as they later came to be called. His idea, like a river, is fed by many rivulets, springs, and streams. Planned towns have been built for various purposes by all civilizations throughout history. The gist of Howard's much misunderstood and misrepresented proposal was not so much to plan towns as to plan the renewal of industrial London and urban growth.

Howard recognized, as American urban renewers in the 1950s and '60s did not, that before a slum is torn down, there must be another place for the slum dwellers to live. He would settle them, along with anyone else who wanted to move out of London, in new communities. He would equip the new towns with industry, so that the residents would have jobs without commuting.

He also recognized, as the American public is now beginning to see, that cities cannot expand wantonly all over the countryside if the advantages of city and country are to be maintained. He would therefore concentrate the city's overspill in his new towns, build a new town all around a city, connect them with the city and one another by rapid transit, and contain both the new towns and the old city within permanent greenbelts to preserve as much open country as possible.

Howard began thinking about this scheme after his return to London in 1876. The poverty and miseries of the new industrial proletariat had begun to impress themselves on many minds. The late Victorian intelligentsia studied and debated the proposals of socialists, Fabians, nationalizers, single-taxers, radicals, and other reformers.

Howard was particularly inspired by Edward Bellamy's *Looking Backward, 2000-1886*. Published in 1888, this utopian romance describes a Communist Boston in the Year 2000. Howard helped import the book to England. "I determined to take such part as I could to bring a new civilization into being," he said later.

Howard's own, brief book was published in 1898 with the help of a £50 subsidy supplied by a friend. Entitled *Tomorrow: A Peaceful Path to Real Reform*, it was an instant success. A new edition, with the title *Garden Cities of Tomorrow*, was published in 1902. The little book is still in print in many languages.

Tomorrow is an endearing combination of high-flown idealism and sober practicality. It is illustrated with diagrams that have been reproduced in thousands of urban planning books.

The first diagram shows three magnets. One represents the Town. It offers, writes Howard, "the advantages of high wages, opportunities for employment, tempting prospects of advancement, but these are largely counterbalanced by high rents and prices. Its social opportunities and its places of amusement are very alluring, but excessive hours of toil, distance from work, and 'the isolation of crowds' tend greatly to reduce the value of these good things. The well-lit streets are a great attraction, especially in winter, but the sunlight is being more and more shut out, while the air is so vitiated that the fine public buildings like the sparrows, rapidly become covered with soot, and the very statues are in despair. Palatial edifices and fearful slums are the strange, complementary features of modern cities."

The Country magnet, in contrast, "declares itself to be the source of all beauty and wealth; but the Town magnet mockingly reminds her that she is very dull for lack of society, and very sparing of her gifts for lack of capital. There are in the country beautiful vistas, lordly parks, violet-scented woods, fresh air, sounds of rippling water; but too often one sees those threatening words, 'Trespassers will be prosecuted'. . . .

"But neither the Town magnet nor the Country magnet represents the full plan and purpose of nature. Human society and the beauty of nature are meant to be enjoyed together. The two magnets must be made one. . .

"Town and country *must be married,* and out of this joyous union will spring a new hope, a new life, a new civilization."

Howard's new civilization was to be launched on a 6,000-acre piece of real estate costing £40 an acre, or £240,000, at an interest not exceeding 4 percent. It was to be purchased cooperatively by interested citizens, mainly prospective residents and industrialists of Garden City.

The "joyous union of town and country" is illustrated in diagrams. In the center of Garden City, which Howard thought should have a population of about 30,000, he shows a park with ample recreation grounds, town hall, concert and lecture hall, theater, library, museum, and hospital. Running all around the Central Park is a wide glass arcade called the "Crystal Palace," an enclosed shopping mall. Surrounding the Crystal Palace are rings of "excellently built houses, each standing on its own ample grounds . . . . of very varied architecture and design."

All this is further encircled by the stately Grand Avenue, along which yet another park is to be found, containing churches and schools with their playgrounds. On the outer ring of the town are factories, warehouses, dairies, markets, coal yards, timber yards, and such, served by a spur of the railway to London, approximately 30 miles distant.

Beyond the industrial belt is the greenbelt, still part of the 6,000-acre property, devoted to large farms, small farms, small holdings, allotments, cow pastures, and whatever else is green and pleasant. This agricultural belt, providing produce and fresh air for the town's residents, houses another 2,000 people.

Howard's detractors, basing their judgment on a simplistic reading of the diagrams, have called the new towns regimented, dull, and simplistic. They chose to overlook Howard's repeated warning in his book that his diagrams and descriptions are merely suggestive and that actual plans cannot be drawn until there is an actual site.

The detractors, often Modernists and their drummers, also say that Howard's concept is anticity and thus, of course, horribly bumpkin. They obviously have not read his book and did not even look at Howard's diagram number five "illustrating correct principles of a city's growth—open country ever near at hand, and rapid communication between offshoots."

As the new cities are being built, Howard says, London can be transformed. "Elsewhere the town is invading the country; here the country must invade the town." As workers flock to the new industries, their slum housing can give way to parks and open space. "New systems of railways, sewerage, drainage, lighting can be constructed to save London. The whole system of production and distribution can undergo changes as complete and as remarkable as was the change from a system of barter to our present complicated commercial system."

"The time," says Howard, "for the complete reconstruction of London—which will eventually take place on a far more comprehensive scale than that now exhibited in Paris, Berlin, Glasgow, Birmingham, or Vienna—has, however, not yet come. A simpler problem must first be solved. One small Garden City must be built as a working model, and then a group of cities. . . ."

Using rapid transit, inhabitants of one town in the cluster, as another diagram shows, can reach another town or the central city in a few minutes. The regional cluster thus would represent one community. "Each inhabitant of the whole group, though in one sense living in a town of a small size, would be in reality living in, and would enjoy the advantages of, a great and most beautiful city."

The greenbelt around towns and city brings "all the fresh

delights of the country—field, hedgerow, and woodland—not prim parks and gardens merely—within a few minutes' walk or ride."

If this is antiurban, it certainly is urbane. In contrast to the Modern movement that engendered popular hostility, Howard's vision aroused immediate enthusiasm.

Within months after Howard's *Peaceful Path* was published, the Garden City Association, now known as the Town and Country Planning Association, started blazing the trail.

The association resolved early not to be committed "to any of Mr. Howard's suggestions with regard to details, its object being to carry out the general principles advocated by him with the assistance of the best available advice and assistance."

Advice and assistance soon became available as the group was joined by business and professional men as well as an impressive number of influential public figures. By 1902, the association boasted 1,000 members. In June of that year, at a meeting in the Crown Room of the Holborn Restaurant in London, with Earl Grey in the chair, it was agreed to take the decisive first step.

The Garden City Pioneer Company was registered with a capital of £20,000. Within four months of the issue of the prospectus, four months of hectic activity among educational, social, political, cooperative, religious and temperance societies, the capital was fully subscribed.

Soon the audience of Shaw's *John Bull's Other Island* heard one character ask another: "Have you heard of Garden City?"

"D'ye mean Heav'n?"

"No. It's near Hitchin."

And sure enough, there it was, in Hertfordshire, 35 miles from London—Letchworth, the first garden city, thoughtfully designed by Raymond Unwin and his partner, Barry Parker.

Letchworth today is a thriving town. Its population has reached its prescribed limit of 30,000. It has worked out pretty much as Howard had hoped, a verdant, tranquil place that has become a community. The greenbelt has not prevented the town from stimulating the economy of the surrounding, rural countryside.

Yet, Letchworth might be regarded as a lone, somewhat quaint, utopian experiment, had Howard not ventured a second demonstration of his concept with the aid of a younger group of associates. The second garden city, Welwyn, also in Hertfordshire, but only 20 miles from King's Cross Station in London, was begun in 1919. The plan by Louis de Soissons is more lively and varied than that of Letchworth.

Compared to the daring, often brazen sculptural experiments of the Abstractionists, the architecture of both these first new towns, as of most of those that were to follow, is conventional. It's old shoe. But residents and visitors are comfortable with it.

The new town movement does not concern itself with fashionable form. It is concerned with function, with the workings of community life in the modern age. It is concerned with easy access to work, recreation, and cultural stimulation, with making it safe for children to walk to school, and with making it easy for parents to push baby carriages when they go shopping. It is concerned with keeping traffic and noise under control. It is concerned, in short, with making use of modern technology without sacrificing the social advantages of the historic city.

In all of this, Letchworth and Welwyn probably offer more important promises for humanistic architecture than the experiments of abstract aesthetics at Weissenhof, let alone Pessac.

Missing in Letchworth and Welwyn are parking spaces. The new town design for the motor age, like the motor age itself, came from the United States.

15 The Clean Dream

America first learned of Howard's peaceful path as it entered World War I.

The federal government, under Woodrow Wilson, searched for efficient ways to provide housing for munitions and shipyard workers. The search led to England, where American architects discovered new town design, particularly that of Raymond Unwin, which had been inspired by the Garden City movement. Glowing reports were published in the *Journal of the American Institute of Architects*. Letchworth and other Unwin projects soon inspired several federally sponsored war housing communities in this country.

The AIA *Journal* articles and discussions also brought a group of exceptional people together who, in 1923, formed the Regional Planning Association of America.

It was not, as the somewhat officious name might lead you to assume, another idealistic organization with lofty aims and lofty names, grinding out unreadable studies and unread press releases.

It was an association of friends—the friends of Lewis Mumford.

Mumford's group, a branch, so to speak, of the English Town and Country Planning Association, believed in regional planning as a means of achieving urban order, and in urban order as a means of achieving a reasonably civilized society.

Mumford, writer and social critic, is, in the phrase his friend Sir Frederic Osborn applied to himself, "a specialist on things in general." He began his career as a student of biology. Under the influence of Geddes, he soon became interested in the urban ecology. This, in turn, attracted him to Howard's concepts that Clarence Stein and others wrote about in the AIA *Journal.*

Most members of Mumford's group, which held together for a decade, were architects and city planners. Clarence Stein, working with Henry Wright, was foremost among them. Other illustrious members of the group included Benton Mackaye and Catherine Bauer Wurster.

Mackaye, the forester and regional planner, proposed the Appalachian Trail and was the foremost planner of the Tennessee Valley Authority and the Rural Electrification Administration. Ahead of his time, he proposed public control of urbanization to assure that development is related to natural resources, energy, and commodity flow, in order to avoid congestion, traffic jams, maldistribution and environmental pollution. He proposed a highway system that would bypass human settlements rather than disrupt them, as our federal highway program has done.

Catherine Bauer Wurster was by profession a writer on housing and city planning, and by temperament a Joan of Arc in the cause of housing America's future. Tireless and persuasive, she had considerable influence on U.S. urban policy in the 1930s, '40s, and '50s.

In Mumford's words, the group was devoted to "the vivid interchange of the ideas of Geddes and Howard, the economic analyses of Thorstein Veblen, the sociology of Charles Horton Cooley, and the educational philosophy of John Dewey, to say nothing of the new ideas in conservation, ecology, and geotechnics . . .

"It made up in intensity what it lacked in extension. A core of members met at least two or three times each week, sometimes more, for lunch or dinner, and from time to time somewhat more formal meetings were held over a weekend at the Hudson Guild Farm in Netcong, New Jersey, for strenuous systematic discussions. (The members came with their wives and incidentally were among the first urban groups to revive the square dances and the Appalachian folk ballads.)"

Out of the discussions came numerous articles and books, which in turn, led to more conferences and discussions. In time, an increasing number of government and planning officials attended. Sometimes the meetings heard leaders of the new town movement from England, including, in 1924, Ebenezer Howard himself.

"After the First World War," Clarence Stein wrote, "there was a strong surge of enthusiasm for a better world . . . New York's great Democratic governor, Al Smith, planned to replace the slums in which he had grown up. As a result, there was created the Commission of Housing and Regional Planning. He made me chairman. Up to that time in America, our attack on housing had been regulatory—legal don'ts. I went abroad in search of more constructive action. In England, 'new towns' . . . were attempting to chart a new way; the second garden city, Welwyn, was being built."

The final report of Governor Smith's commission, according to Mumford, "was so farsighted and far-reaching that, some 40 years later, it still served as the basis for a similar project by Governor Rockefeller's Office of Regional Development" published in 1965. Later it served as the basis for the work of the New York State Urban Development Corporation.

With Mumford and others cheering them on, Clarence Stein and Henry Wright first built Sunnyside Gardens, a community for 1,200 moderate-income families on Long Island. Stein and Wright also designed Chatham Village in Pittsburgh. And, toward the end of his life, Stein planned Kimitat, a new town in British Columbia.

Stein and Wright's most seminal design, a breakthrough in city planning, was Radburn, New Jersey, a town planned for 25,000 people.

Begun in 1928, Radburn was to be a complete garden city, much as Howard had conceived it. But it was also to be a town, as Stein put it, "in which people could live peacefully with the automobile—or rather in spite of it." Radburn was the first urban design with a complete separation of pedestrians and automobiles. You see its influence in every new settlement where the children can be let outdoors without fear of being run over by trucks.

Stein placed the backside of the houses along service lanes that lead to secondary collector roads around his superblocks. These, in turn, are linked to the main roads that connect various neighborhoods and connect with the highways and parkways.

The fronts of the houses face a common—a publicly shared park within the superblock. The walkways to school and to the community and shopping centers are separated from the motorways by underpasses.

The essence of Radburn's livability is that in every detail of its design, the aim is not to make the most economical use of the land, but the most economical use of people—protecting them from the abrasive effects of noise, poisoned air, needless tensions, fears, and alienation. Stein's ingenious plan proved that this is technically possible without any sacrifice of mechanical comforts. Cars are parked at every house (but don't obstruct the family patio). There are electric refrigerators, dehumidifiers and knife sharpeners, to say nothing of television sets—just as everywhere in America's vast suburbs. And yet the machines do not dominate. The place is, as Mumford said, "deeply human."

The first home owners moved into Radburn in May 1929, five months before the stock market collapsed. The corporation was ruined in the Great Depression. It lost most of the land beyond what it had already developed. But the Radburn idea lives on as one of the foremost architectural innovations of the twentieth century.

Today, the small part of the town that was completed still functions as an active community. It consists of 638 single family homes, or about 3,000 people, 50 duplex apartments, 100 apartments, a shopping center, a community center, playgrounds, and parks. The community and recreation activities are managed by a full-time staff of six people, supervised by the elected officers of the Radburn Association.

The Radburn Association maintains a park network of 23 acres, two swimming pools, four tennis courts, three baseball fields, three playground areas, five outdoor basketball courts, an archery plaza, two pavilions, hundreds of yards of walkway, a walkway lighting system, the most photographed underpass in the world, and a community center for movies, amateur theater, a library, and other activities. All this is in fine condition and financed by an assessment that may not exceed half of the municipal taxes. Despite the special assessment, Radburn's 1929 houses sell for many thousands of dollars more than comparable houses in nearby communities. (The same is true of the low-cost, workers' housing built under the New Deal in greenbelt towns.)

This is largely due to the power and durability of good design. Karl J. Ingebritsen, who specializes in community management, found in a recent study that the Radburn Association also has a great deal to do with "the survival of Radburn as a viable, popular, and distinctive entity in congested northern New Jersey."

At the time Radburn was built, Governor Franklin D. Roosevelt spoke at a meeting of the Regional Planning Association and was familiar with its ideas. He remembered them when he moved to Pennsylvania Avenue. For all its concern with banking and securities, agriculture, and, most of all, jobs, the New Deal understood better than any national effort before or after, that the nation's welfare is inseparably connected with the welfare of its land and natural resources. The watchword of the time was "conservation," and many took that to mean only the silence of wild forests and prairies. But much of what Franklin Roosevelt attempted also deals with cities and city living, and what, for lack of a more attractive term, we call the "built environment." It adds up to a comprehensive national environmental policy that must now be reclaimed, updated, and put to work.

One of the most important features of that policy was the National Planning Board, later named the National Resources

Planning Board. Under Interior Secretary Harold Ickes, it coordinated the work of State Planning Boards that were set up in all but one state. Among other things, these boards directed the activities of the Civilian Conservation Corps that provided useful work and vocational training for unemployed young men, who went on to build hiking trails and nature parks across the country, as well as such special projects as the delightful Paseo del Rio, the riverside walkway that meanders through the city of San Antonio.

The CCC is gone, but the New Deal's Tennessee Valley Authority remains as one of America's greatest accomplishments. It achieved lower electricity rates and higher incomes that turned a depressed region into a valley of prosperous farms and impressive industrial growth: the TVA instituted flood control that tamed destructive rivers with a system of 32 major dams, and opened 650 miles of waterways to navigation. And its new recreation and vacation areas along 10,000 miles of lake shore are used by some 50 million people a year.

Its success rests on the combination of all this, on its total ecological approach to an entire region. The TVA made conservation a means of achieving progress. It is dedicated "to use the earth for the good of man," as conservationist Gifford Pinchot put it.

This is not to say that TVA was or is infallible. One of its more glaring mistakes was to condone strip mining—buying coal from mining companies that raped the hills, a practice no less contemptible for having been legal at the time.

However, Aubrey Wagner, retired chairman of TVA's board

of directors and a devoted conservationist, went out of his way to show me strip mining scars, still bleeding with poisonous sulphur rivulets, when he took me on a three-day tour of the Tennessee Valley some years ago. At that time I had not heard of this particular environmental atrocity. Wagner deplored it and wanted me to deplore it in print, long before environmentalists made an issue of it.

Roosevelt had planned similar valley authorities for America's other great rivers. But for the politics of the Corps of Engineers, all our valleys could be clean and clear today, as well as prosperous. We could be swimming in America's rivers.

Mumford's Regional Planning Association did not only supply the ideological basis for all this. Its members and friends were directly engaged in designing the TVA towns, built for the workers who constructed hydroelectric dams—Norris, Wheeler, and Pickwick Landing. The designs followed Clarence Stein's examples and Ebenezer Howard's ideas, including the un-American notion of limiting growth with a permanent greenbelt. The enthusiasm for sound, humane planning even held up when Oak Ridge was hurriedly built during World War II as a secret company town for the Manhattan project that produced the atomic bomb. It is still a pleasant town.

And so, to this day, are the "greenbelt towns"—Greenbelt, Maryland, near Washington, D.C.; Greendale, near Milwaukee; and Greenhills, near Cincinnati—built by the New Deal's Resettlement Administration as experimental model communities for workers' families, as Howard had proposed. They, too, were inspired and largely planned by Clarence Stein, Henry Wright, and the rest of Lewis Mumford's little band.

Greenbelt, Maryland, consists of plain row houses built along landscaped inner courts, where children can play safe from cars. The walkways lead to the shopping center without crossing a motor road. There are still recreation and community activities, and today the town is more popular with its residents than ever. The people who live there chose simple homes in an attractive community over gadget-loaded homes in a fancy subdivision.

When the first families moved into Greenbelt in 1937, they found a lake stocked with fish, athletic fields, a swimming pool and a youth center waiting for them. The movie opened a year later with Shirley Temple in "Little Miss Broadway." Almost everything was run cooperatively.

Roosevelt-haters, conservatives, and latter-day know-nothings riled against TVA and the greenbelt towns. Anything that was not planned exclusively for private profit was denounced as a particularly vicious version of Godless socialism or communism. The notion that any kind of land use and city planning is somehow unpatriotic still lingers on.

If this notion were anything but illiterate, we ought to lower the flag over St. Augustine, Florida; San Antonio, Texas, and its Alamo; Jamestown and Williamsburg, Virginia; Philadelphia; virtually all the New England towns and cities; and, first and foremost, Washington, D.C., our capital. They were all carefully planned along ancient European traditions.

We tell our children nothing about this. Elementary schools teach them how warblers build their nests, but tell not a word about how houses and human settlements are built. Buffalo Bill is a romantic hero in our schools, presumably for killing thousands of buffalo, while Frederick Law Olmsted remains unsung, although he created hundreds of parks all over America.

This illiteracy about our habitat is at once the cause and the result of the country's long indifference toward urban planning. As we fought our way out of the depression, we experimented with new towns, regional and national planning, conservation, and other means of making progress work for livability. We felt that we had "a rendezvous with destiny," as Franklin D. Roosevelt said. This optimism included "the clean dream," as someone called it, the dream of cities and factories as fresh and beautiful as prairies and mountains.

When World War II was over, that dream was forgotten. So

was whatever we had learned at Radburn, the greenbelt towns, and the Tennessee Valley. A feverish, suburban boom swept over the country. The American lessons were learned in England.

16 Essays in Civilization

Hitler's Luftwaffe probably helped as much as Howard's persuasiveness to make the garden city idea Britain's national policy. The New Towns Act was passed in 1946.

Before World War II, Letchworth and Welwyn, although much discussed and admired, had failed to spark the galaxy of satellite towns for which Howard had hoped. While their tidy livability clearly demonstrated that there is an alternative to either city stress or suburban tedium, these first two privately financed garden cities also showed that building a town all at once is a complex and risky business. As American developers were to learn to their sorrow 50 years later, it takes a long time and a lot of money until cash begins to flow in the right direction. Like battleships, wilderness parks, power dams, or park benches, new towns are not investments that prove private enterprise more profitable than public enterprise.

Sir Ebenezer Howard died in 1928, a knighted celebrity. His associate, Frederic Osborn, had taken the torch, lighting fires all over the country, lecturing, debating, studying, pamphleteering, and politicking. But it was not until Nazi bombs started raining on London that the government, forced to consider the dispersal of industry, began to pay attention to Osborn's Town and Country Planning Association. A commission headed by Sir Anthony Montague Barlow proposed that industries and their workers be moved to new satellite towns. It recommended that a national planning authority be chartered to build them.

As war damage mounted, Sir Patrick Abercrombie, the eminent architect-planner, was asked to draw a plan for the reconstruction of London. He proposed to surround the city with a permanent greenbelt (it is still there and green), and designated the location of ten new towns that were to reduce inner-city congestion.

Yet another commission, headed by Lord Reith—who had almost single-handedly created the British Broadcasting Corporation—was charged with working out the administrative and planning mechanisms. A week after the Reith proposals became law, the first new town, Stevenage in Hertfordshire, was launched. "The destruction of war," reflected Patrick Abercrombie, "made us reconsider our whole environment."

Today, a third of a century later, there are 34 new towns in Britain, housing more than two million people and providing jobs for nearly one million residents. Four towns have reached the population for which they were planned. Four more are approaching completion, if a living organism such as a town can ever be said to approach that state. Several towns increased their originally planned size.

The first 14 new British towns—the first generation—were designed to accommodate what the British call the "overspill" populations of London, Glasgow, and other cities. Letchworth and Welwyn, taken over by the government under the New Towns Act, are counted among them. They are located sufficiently distant from the city to discourage commuting, yet close enough for outings among the bright city lights.

A second generation of new towns was planned in the early 1960s, after a pause during which the Conservatives, who had come to power, considered and reaffirmed the idea. This second batch was conceived as regional growth centers. They were to be catalysts for the concentration of new subdivisions, industrial plants, and shopping centers, which in America, sprawl all over the landscape. These second generation towns were planned for populations of 100,000 or more, and are located further away from the old center cities.

The third generation are new communities consisting of expanded old towns, such as Northhampton and Peterborough, expected to house as many as a quarter of a million people.

The most interesting in this group is Milton Keynes, designed by Lord Richard Llewelyn-Davies, who also planned new towns in the United States. It is an experiment in planning a metropolitan area rather than a planned town. It is a regional city comprising several existing villages, of which Milton Keynes, 45 miles from the heart of London, midway between Oxford and Cambridge, is only one. This new city was conceived to accommodate the population growth and industrialization of southeast England so it would not pollute breathing space for millions of people.

The plan provides a grid of primary roads, approximately one kilometer apart. About 5,000 people are to live in each of the resulting squares and each division is to have one or two centers of activity. The idea is for planners to lay down only the necessary fixed elements of the town—the roads, sewers, and water mains, or what they call the infrastructure—without predetermining the size, shape, and purpose of buildings too far in advance of needs and economic considerations. This way there is more flexibility and freedom of choice. Changing tastes and requirements in housing, shopping, transportation, education, and recreation can be more easily accommodated. The aim is to avoid sterility and offer a multiplicity of choices for a variety of social and racial groups.

As presently conceived, however, Milton Keynes, designed for a population of 250,000 people by the end of this century, returns to the low densities, separate neighborhoods, and green and pleasant openness of the early garden cities. We have come full circle.

It is marvelous how, in 30 years of building new towns, the British have managed to learn from mistakes and, in various ways, to improve design and management. Their new towns are indeed, as Lord Reith has called them, "essays in civilization." The key to the success of these essays—and they are a howling success—is that the New Town Act of 1946 created a system of land controls that was revolutionary.

The land is controlled and the new towns are built by the national government through the Ministry of Town and Country Planning. The minister "designates" each new town and its location. He appoints a Development Corporation for each town that purchases the land, draws up the plans and runs the town. When a site, or a number of sites, are under consideration, the land price is frozen so that there can be no land speculation.

The national government supplies the funds, some in the form of grants, but primarily in 60-year loans. The towns are therefore never in danger of running out of funds in the critical investment stage of their development. Loans are repaid by the Development Corporation at the prevailing interest rates from the town's revenues. All British new towns are repaying their loans on schedule, and the government is beginning to profit. Early in 1978, eight New Town Development Corporations started to transfer their assets to elected town councils. They will cease to exist by 1980.

The corporations have considerable freedom for initiative and independent judgment. They suffer none of the paranoid restrictions and strangling red tape our federal government has imposed on new town developers. They built the roads, sewers, and other utilities, and much of the subsidized housing. Recently, much of the new town land is leased for 99 years to private developers who build housing, commercial, and industrial buildings to corporation specifications. The corporations vary in quality and resourcefulness. Some are deemed too cautious. There might be, critics say, more social innovation and experimentation.

While the new town population is fairly representative of the socioeconomic composition of the British population as a whole, they have not relieved the cities of caring for the elderly and the poor in sufficient measure. Instead, they have attracted the young and skilled, whom the old cities are reluctant to lose.

Nor have the British new towns relieved congestion in the cities, to make room for the rebuilding for which Howard had hoped. This is due to the fact that industry and population have expanded faster than the rate of new towns built. More will undoubtedly be launched over the next two decades.

But the new towns did help orderly urban development. They have concentrated urban growth, preserving open country around London and other big cities. The greenbelts have remained green.

This is not to say that Britain does not have its share of ugly billboards, bulldozed landmarks, and other forms of "progress." But it is in better control of its environment than any other industrialized country. The fish are back in the Thames. Birds are singing, and transistor radios are banned in Hyde Park.

Most important, in the words of one British critic, the British new towns "have undoubtedly been successful in creating communities in which people are happy to live." Opinion survey after survey confirms this view.

Britain's new communities look and feel as different from one another as the old ones that developed more slowly. They are certainly more varied and visually interesting than the jerrybuilt industrial towns of the late nineteenth century, or the postwar suburbs of America.

Letchworth and Welwyn are romantic and rustic. Stevenage and Basildon, in the London orbit, are architecturally more adventuresome, although the homes are, by American standards, Spartan. An abundance of landscaped and well-tended walkways, playgrounds, and small parks make up for the dull domesticity. The town centers are dramatic stage sets, more dramatic than the best shopping centers in the United States. Stevenage's center is no Piazza dei Signori in Verona, and Basildon's center no Piazza Roma in Urbino. But the British places, too, attract people and pigeons just for the pleasure of being there.

Only one of the British new towns actually *looks* new—and startling. The design is original, ingenious, and intriguing. I was

quite taken by Cumbernauld. It was built in the early sixties on
rolling Scottish hills, 14 miles northeast of Glasgow. In contrast
to the verdant pleasantries and familiarity of the other towns, it
is urban and strange. It has some high-rise apartments and a
predominance of tightly packed row houses. The average
density is 85.5 persons per acre. Most walkways and playgrounds are paved with the granite cobblestones disposed of by
the city of Glasgow.

Cumbernauld's town center is a beehive megastructure,
consisting of enclosed shopping malls, offices, apartments, and
a theatrical array of ramps, gallerias, and terraces. It looks like
a bizarre battleship, gliding through Scotland's foggy hills.

The point is that the structure straddles a highway that
divides the town. As the town grows along the highway, so will
the center megastructure, so that no resident will ever live more
than half a mile or so from the pubs and bustle. There is parking
under the center and outdoors games on its top. The odor of
fish 'n' chips pervades the ramps and stairs. There is neon
advertising and there are clusters of teenagers. The indoor
shopping mall is a bit gloomy but not half as gloomy as the
Scottish outdoors can be at times.

Cumbernauld separates cars and people more completely
than any other town. A network of footpaths is never crossed
by a motorized wheel. There are hardly any traffic accidents.

What makes the new town new and different from both cities
and suburbs are a few basic planning principles.

The foremost of these is to create a place with a clear identity,
where people of different incomes and backgrounds and ages
can live, play, shop, learn, worship, frolic, and raise children.

Another is that the settlement, whatever its size, is made up of
a number of small neighborhoods where people can walk to buy
a loaf of bread, take their young to a daycare center or
elementary school, find some outdoor recreation, and perhaps
have a drink in a congenial bar.

A third basic principle is communion with nature. No matter
how urban the place, there ought to be a garden, or at least a
patio, for everyone. There must be plenty of trees alive with

birds. Natural features, such as hills and brooks, are respected and enhanced rather than bulldozed. In America, man-made lakes have become a new town trademark.

Since Clarence Stein and the Radburn plan, a final, essential planning principle is to keep people and cars apart. Surprisingly, this still seems a revolutionary idea. No one would think of building homes directly along busy railroad tracks. Yet there is still no outcry against living, walking, and playing on dangerous, noisy and polluted motor roads—against turning streets into parking lots. Cars are allowed to roam where no decent horse had ever dared to trot.

In Britain, these practical planning principles, rather than aesthetic predilections, tend to determine the design of new town architecture. More often than not, this architecture is undistinguished—not as humdrum as the mass of America's suburban builder homes, nor as conspicuous as the "good architecture" modern critics will notice. Which is why some of these critics still denounce the new towns as dull. "Why that's where everybody commits suicide," a famous architect once told me in earnest.

Yet for all its plainness, the design of Britain's new town

buildings serves the needs of community better than the look-alike high-rise apartments of the new towns of France and the socialist countries; better, too, than Swedish new town architecture with its mix of high and low buildings.

The most consistently attractive modern new town architecture is in Tapiola, near Helsinki, in Finland. But Tapiola's buildings are not conspicuous either. High fashion design—clever styling—is not what a good community needs.

The new architecture that is beginning to emerge responds to the requirements of community and the human and natural ecology. It is simple, soft-spoken, and natural.

17 Instant Portofino

With all their abstract funk and functionalism, as Forrest Wilson calls it, American architecture and planning professors of the 1940s and '50s paid no attention to what was happening in Great Britain. If the subject came up at all, experts and idiots alike denounced the British accomplishments. I doubt that the words Riverside or Radburn were ever mentioned in the architecture and planning schools of those years—years in which we built the equivalent of one brand new Chicago every year. Surely the zoning officials and suburban developers who shaped most of this building never thought of the long-range economic and ecological consequences of suburbanizing all of the continent's shores along the Pacific, Atlantic, and the Great Lakes.

One of the very few planned communities worthy of the name was Park Forest, some 30 miles from the Chicago Loop. Designed in 1947 for a population of 30,000 (Howard's ideal size), it offered a mixture of row houses, single family houses, and apartments, some for rent. The community included a shopping center and reserved land for schools, parks, churches, playgrounds, and other attributes of civilized life that make no direct profit for the developer.

The developer was Phillip M. Klutznick, one of the public housers of the New Deal days. He was assisted by Elmer Peets, the landscape architect and urban designer, and Henry

Churchill, the architect. Both moved in the intellectual orbit of Clarence Stein and each had a hand in the greenbelt towns.

The modest fame of Park Forest was soon eclipsed by the Levittowns, no doubt the apogee of America's suburban civilization. The secret of their success is that builders Levitt & Sons applied basic mass production and marketing techniques to homebuilding. In the first town on Long Island, early in the 1950s, Levitt built 15,000 identical houses in less than three years and sold them for $8,000, and later, $9,000 apiece. Like the Model T Ford, they are a good product.

To accelerate the cash flow, Levitt wrapped the houses in an economy-size community package. He donated land for schools and built ten neighborhood parks, nine swimming pools, and a community hall. Nine pools and a hall are, of course, not excessive for 92,000 residents. There is, in fact, not much to do in Levittown, except mow the lawn and raise children. Teenagers took to vandalism. There were traffic and transportation problems, and strained relations with the Nassau county government.

But there are always traffic problems, bored teenagers, and touchy county councilmen. It was easy for intellectuals to complain that our affluence might buy us more than boredom and cookie cutter cottages with television antennae. It was silly for architects to complain that Levitt should have applied designs and a technology more sophisticated than houses nailed together by teams instead of single carpenters. But Levitt knew that nobody wants to live in abstract designs and a sophisticated technology—except perhaps astronauts traveling through space.

The fact is that middle-income, middle-aged Levittowners seem happy and, by and large, unresponsive to the needs even of their own children, let alone what might be called "cultural values." Most of them, including sociologist Herbert Gans, who lived in a Levittown long enough to write a euphoric defense of it, consider it a modern Garden of Eden. For many residents, Levittown was the first, exhilarating rung on the ladder of upward mobility. Released from the city tenements, they had wall-to-wall carpeting, all-electric kitchens with laundromats (and without cockroaches), plus safe yards to give baby an airing. Nobody told them that Eden might be improved if there were sidewalks, if the overhead wiring might be buried, if there were a neighborhood center with a sculpture and a library, if walkways and motorways were separated. For thoughtful intellectuals, to be sure, the Lower East Side had more "ambience." But Levittown was not built for thoughtful intellectuals. Mies van der Rohe's Lafayette Park in Detroit or Gropiusstadt in West Berlin would no more win a beauty contest in Levittown than a Levitt house could win a Museum of Modern Art competition.

But then, suddenly, in 1964, a new and different urban vision appeared on American television news and feature shows and in the picture magazines. It clearly bridged the culture gap, appealing both to elite aestheticism and popular nostalgia. It conveyed a sense of the good life that was, for a change, not an advertising writer's phantasmagoria. Reston's Lake Anne Village Center is as real as Times Square or the Washington Monument.

Reston and Columbia are the first and most advanced of the spate of American new towns that sprouted in the late 1960s and seemed to wither in the drought of the Nixon administration. Reston is in Virginia, about 20 miles south of Washington. Columbia is in Maryland, midway between Washington and Baltimore. Both towns are the creation of exceptional individuals: Reston's Robert E. Simon, Jr., who gave his initials to the name of his town, and Columbia's James W. Rouse, who held a public contest for the name of his enterprise.

Both are idealists as well as entrepreneurs. Simon would improve the way people live. Rouse would improve people.

Both are also good examples of my contention that, for the creation of a good habitat, good clients are just as important, if not more so, than good architects. Columbia has no spectacular, avant-garde architecture. It nevertheless pioneers a new way of life. Restonians have told me they love their town because it's so beautiful. Columbians praise Columbia for being so friendly.

Reston is laid out on 7,000 acres of rolling woods and

farmland in Fairfax County, Virginia. Simon conceived it to be almost like a country club where you walk to the tennis court, riding stables, and golf course. He would talk about the problems with youth and provided a "Rathskeller" for teenagers. He would talk about culture and arranged adult education courses and an art gallery.

In accordance with Clarence Stein's concepts, children were to be able to walk to school, and adults to essential shopping, without crossing a motor road. In accordance with Ebenezer Howard's concepts, people were to live and work in the same community. Reston has a thriving, 970-acre industrial park with light industry, offices, and a conference center close to Dulles Airport for people who want to meet between jets.

Less hectic people should be able to stay put all their lives if they wish, Simon said, so he provided both family co-ops and single nests in the same neighborhood. The dignity of the individual was foremost in Simon's mind. Reston was to be a place of beauty.

Surprisingly, and despite much adversity, it is. Simon and his architects spent an inordinate amount of money and care on achieving excellence. There are flowers and carefully swept walkways everywhere. Even the pedestrian underpasses under the motor road are wide, well-lit and adorned with simple sculpture. It was important, Simon told me, to set the right tone, to start with a high standard of quality. It would never do to start modestly in hopes of improving the quality of his buildings and landscaping later. For that reason, Simon, though he had every honest intention of including residents of all incomes, built for the well-to-do first "so that we can provide the amenities and services everyone ought to have."

This ambition soon bankrupted Simon. But it did set standards that even a pragmatic, profit-minded corporation like Gulf Oil, which took over from Simon, felt compelled to live up to with relatively minor compromises. Although not everyone would wish to live in Reston (wouldn't it be awful if everyone wanted to live in the same kind of place?), Simon and his architects have shown us that our age can achieve as much livability as any other.

The Reston masterplan was prepared by Whittlesey, Conklin and Rossant, who also designed the Lake Anne Village Center. In addition to Lake Anne, the town plan calls for six other villages, each with its market place, school, community center, church, and, of course, swimming pool, tennis court, and other recreation.

A town center, much like a regional shopping center, was to serve not only the 75,000 residents Reston hopes to accomodate, but also some 50,000 people in the surrounding region. But that hope was dashed when, for lack of comprehensive regional planning, a huge and hideous shopping center, Tyson's Corner, was allowed to mushroom only seven miles from Reston.

Reston's showpiece is Lake Anne. The lake is man-made but looks natural, except for a dramatic water jet spraying the sky. On a nice day there are small sailboats and canoes on the lake. Motorboats are blissfully absent.

Some of the residents who live along the lake go shopping in their canoes, mooring them on a marina along the town plaza. The plaza is defined by a crescent shaped row of stores with balconied apartments above them and a sculptural fountain in front. There is also a church, with dramatic steps leading up to it, where people sit to chat, overlooking the bustle. Facing the plaza is a good restaurant that puts its tables out in the summer. Off on the side is an apartment tower. It has an art gallery on the

ground floor and, like the Campanile on the Piazza San Marco, seems like an exclamation point in this poetic composition.

The townhouses framing the lake on the west were designed by Chloethiel Woodard Smith. Water laps at their walls, and the boat pier seems to lead right into their living rooms. Their pastel hues recall Portofino. Charles M. Goodman designed the cluster of townhouses in the hilly woods above the lake. The well-composed arrangement of Le Corbusier-inspired houses is set on a terraced platform that covers a parking garage. The houses are white with accents of bright color and sport large windows and terraces, shaded by amiable trellises. The Whittlesey, Conklin and Rossant stores and townhouses are expressive brick structures with a medieval feeling. They are simple, but not plain; unpretentious, but not unassuming. They are of our time: that is, they do not ape the style of any other period, making them "modern," I suppose. But they are not modern with a capital M. It strikes me as utter nonsense—and it was probably damaging to Simon—that real estate writers called them and other Lake Anne architecture "modernistic" and "avant-garde." It surely is neither.

At any rate, Lake Anne or Queen Anne, the much praised first village of Reston, was plagued not by good architecture but by poor economics—slow development and accumulating debt. One trouble was the poor location. Reston has no access to the four-lane freeway between Dulles Airport and downtown Washington. Foremost was the dilemma that later American new towns faced: it takes a huge investment and a long time to start a new community. During the years a developer must spend to build roads and sewers, schools and stores, houses and playgrounds, he has no income. But he must, nevertheless, pay interest on the land and the bills for developing the community. That takes a lot of "patient money."

Robert Simon's lenders got impatient. In a ruthless coup, the Gulf Oil Corporation, in 1967, took over to protect its investment, and ousted Simon. With new investments from Gulf, and several insurance companies, Reston is now a steadily growing community. Among its large employers is the U.S. Geological Survey, a federal agency.

Reston has its fair share of residents of moderate income, living in subsidized housing. With its art, theater, gardening, and adult education activities, it fulfills Ebenezer Howard's promises as well as any English new town. The lyricism of Lake Anne's architecture, however, has not been equalled.

The scene has changed little since I first visited Lake Anne Plaza a dozen or so years ago except, perhaps, that the trees have matured and the fountain, store signs, and buildings have attained a kind of patina. They look less self-conscious.

There are still a lot of young people, because the village square is where the drugstore and the youth center are. Now a few of the youngsters are black. The girls take part in the horseplay. Smaller kids splash around the fountain. A young man reads unperturbed on top of a bollard—Thoreau, no doubt. A few kids sit motionless on the bulkhead, watching their fishing lines. Adults push shopping carts across the pavement. A little girl, called home for supper by her father on one of the balconies, stamps her feet in tearful protest. There is commotion as an elderly gentlemen, assisted by his wife and an excited poodle, ineptly tries to moor his canoe.

I sit in the outdoor cafe and watch as, at other times, I sat and watched the goings-on in the central square in Siena or Burghausen. It seems as though everyone might join hands at any moment and break into the opening chorus.

People do, in fact, hold dances, ceremonies, and pageants at Lake Anne Plaza, as they do on the plazas of other new towns, and the *place de ville, piazza,* and *Marktplatz* of Europe. Reston seems to me to be reconnecting us with our past.

18 The Next America

In Columbia, the stage settings for the human drama are, shall we say, less artistic and therefore less convincing. Columbia is more like a Schlitz than a Chateau Neuf de Pape and there is nothing wrong with a cool Schlitz on a warm day.

James W. Rouse, who unknowingly launched Columbia at the same time Simon launched Reston, was born into a large family on the Eastern Shore of Maryland in 1914. His first job, as a young lawyer, was with the Federal Housing Administration, newly formed at the time. In 1939 he went into the mortgage banking and real estate development business. The fame and fortune of the Rouse Company are built on giant shopping centers all over the country, including the carefully restored Quincy Market in Boston.

Simon started Reston with an aesthetic vision. Rouse started

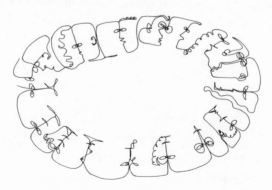

Columbia in hopes of reversing what he called "frantic, fractured living, the loneliness amid the busyness, the rising delinquency among middle-class children, increasing neurosis, alcoholism, divorce, the destruction of nature." He sought salvation in a perhaps naive faith in behavioral science. At regular intervals throughout 1963, he brainstormed with a social scientist, a sociologist, a psychologist, a city manager, a recreation expert, and an educator, as well as his staff of architects and planners.

Perhaps not surprisingly, what emerged from these sessions was the essential scheme of Howard's Garden City, ca. 1920. The chief difference between Columbia and Welwyn is that Columbia is more conventionally suburban and that, while the concept is good, the architecture is not.

The essential scheme starts with a neighborhood of 2,000-5,000 people, built around an elementary school, park and playground, swimming pool, community center building, and, in some cases, a convenience store. In Columbia, unfortunately, it is not the Ma and Pa type, but a Seven Eleven chain store.

Two to four neighborhoods are then combined to form a village of 10,000-15,000 people. The village center, as in the city of old, is the focal point of urban community life. It is the market place (now known as shopping center), the place to see and be seen by others, and the place for cultural activity, recreation, and communal politics. Most of Columbia's village centers have sculpture to give them a sense of place. The architecture could be anyplace.

Columbia's seven villages were planned around an architectural disaster called Columbia's "downtown." It is a boondocks boondoggle. It is hard to conceive that anyone should have actually planned this haphazard array of unsightly buildings.

The buildings house offices, a very good restaurant, and an enormous, enclosed shopping mall that is lively and attractive inside. There are also acres and acres of parking lots, a fat spaghetti of roads, thin vermicelli overpasses with spiral ramps, a sprinkling of green, a terraced amphitheatrical mini-park, assorted over-designed lamp posts, and a lake. A very pretty lake.

The disaster is that all of this is totally disjointed. There is no connection, relationship, interplay or coherence among any of these elements. The only thing down in this "downtown"—so far down that you don't even see it if you're up there shopping in the frozen dust of the air-conditioned mall, or working in any of the faceless office buildings—is the lake. It's a wasted investment.

But this "downtown" is not for people anyway. It's for cars. You must even drive to the next office building 300 yards away, because there are no sidewalks or other pedestrian connections between buildings.

In its earlier days, Columbia was advertised as "the next America." I hope that the next America is more than an egocentric assembly of buildings, and treats its lakes and waterfronts as more than a sideshow—or rather, a road show. Just about the only view you get of Columbia's lake is from Route 29, traveling 55 miles per hour.

If Columbia's "downtown" is architecturally mediocre and antiurban, the rest of the town, designed for a population of 110,000 is pleasantly suburban. The town—and, I suspect, Jim Rouse—is ambivalent about the automobile. On the one hand, Rouse wants to tame the combustion engine. He built separate walkways to the schools and neighborhood centers, and a special lane on the major roads reserved for a future public transportation system. The Columbia Association, the town's quasi-government, also operates a scheduled minibus service. On the other hand, one of the first buildings that opened for business in Columbia was the drive-in bank at Wilde Lake Center. Everywhere, furthermore, Rouse provided ample and inviting parking lots and motor roads. There seems as much blacktop as green turf in Columbia.

This all too familiar scene is deliberately all too familiar. Rouse believes that the essence of a good community are good, innovative public institutions. I am sure he has nothing against good, innovative architecture (he has commissioned some handsome buildings elsewhere), but he told me that he was not going to risk customer acceptance of his social innovations by taking chances on the public's architectural taste.

Columbia's social institutions are impressive. The schools, run by the county but initially endowed with Ford Foundation grants, are exemplary in their designs, as well as their educational programs. The town is racially and economically integrated, with some 20 percent of all housing subsidized for low-income families. About 18 percent of the population is black. Interestingly, the median income of black families is higher than that of nonblacks. The subsidized low-rent housing is well distributed throughout the town in clusters of no more than 100 units that are in inconspicuous parts of each village.

The unique Columbia Park and Recreation Association builds, operates, and maintains public spaces and playfields. Its membership dues are a form of local tax. The Protestant Columbia Cooperative Ministry was formed to seek out new opportunities for community work, the foremost being the administration of some of the low-rent housing. Catholics, Jews, and Protestants share the Interfaith Center located in Wilde Lake Village. The Columbia Medical Plan, a prepaid group practice health care program affiliated with the John Hopkins Medical Institutions, strives to prevent health problems and runs the town's hospital and clinics.

Columbia also has three colleges, art groups representing the interests of painters, dancers, actors, and writers, an open air concert pavilion, a professional dinner theater, and a thriving industrial park that employs nearly 20,000 people.

Columbia, which also had it financial difficulties, seems to grow faster than Reston, and may be financially more successful. I am convinced this is due entirely to its location. Columbia is right at the point where the expanding Washington metropolitan area and the expanding Baltimore metropolitan area are about to collide. Rouse carefully selected the site and began to assemble it before the people of Howard County noted the two-pronged advance of bulldozers. Rouse paid less per acre than Simon.

But it took him a year to assemble his 15,000 acres in 140 small parcels. To avoid speculative price increases, this operation was as super-secret as any the CIA ever undertook. The Howard County councilmen just about fainted as a body when one day in 1963, Rouse announced he owned a tenth of their county.

Rouse is the first to concede that it can never be done again. No private developer will ever be able to assemble enough land to build a new town where it is needed in the regional, social, economic, and ecological scheme of things.

Reston and Columbia are remarkable achievements. They prove that the new town is also valid in America. But they are private real estate ventures built for profit, not "social cities," as Ebenezer Howard conceived them and as America needs them. They are the products of a single man's vision, but successful social cities require regional planning and intelligent government support.

19 Black Man's Hope or Corporate Boon?

What came next, unfortunately, was not James Rouse's "Next America," but the quick rise and agonizing fall of the new town movement in America. It moved on and off the national stage so rapidly that even insiders hardly understood what had happened and why. The public never had a chance to comprehend the meaning and potential of new towns.

With the appearance of Reston and Columbia in the mid-sixties, the new town idea suddenly became fashionable. It was considered good for people, like yoga or yogurt.

Ten years later the whole thing was just as suddenly gone. It was bad for us. It was as though the Food and Drug Administration had found that new towns caused some kind of disease in rats.

In the summer of 1967, when Rouse put his signs to the Next America on Maryland's Route 29, the urban research industry, city planners, big corporations, big city mayors, and several official study commissions predicted great things. The greatest of them was that hundreds of semiskilled sociologists found lucrative jobs making verbose studies of new towns in all their aspects and potentials. City planners by the plane load pilgrimaged to England and Scandinavia to marvel at the wonders, and returned to show trays and trays of slides.

General Electric, Boise Cascade, Westinghouse, Humble Oil, and other giant corporations announced plans for instant

garden cities, sheltering taxes as well as people, and featuring a golf course in every village and a lake at every doorstep. "Private enterprise is moving ahead on the job of building new cities," proclaimed *Nation's Business* in August 1968.

Private enterprise did no such thing. It only discovered, or thought it did, that if you can make money selling subdivision houses, you ought to be able to make even more money if you throw in an industrial park and a country club. Besides, the corporations figured, real estate would be a hedge against inflation.

In the late sixties, business magazines variously reported as many as 140 and even 250 "new towns" underway. Most never got beyond "an architect's rendering" attached to a press release. The rest were subdivisions with community centers, sometimes not even with a store, hawked as "a town," "a city," "a new way of life."

Big city mayors were at first opposed to new towns for fear of losing their remaining industries to them. They changed their minds in 1968, when the inner city ghettos burned, generating much hot air about "the crisis of the cities." New satellite towns, they hoped, might absorb their surplus of poor people.

The federal Department of Housing and Urban Development consequently also changed its mind and gave the new town idea its lukewarm endorsement. Dr. Robert Weaver, the department's first secretary under Kennedy and Johnson, thought it more politic, however, to call new towns "new communities."

The staid Advisory Commission on Intergovernmental Relations showed considerably more warmth in recommending a national new towns policy. Both Hubert Humphrey and Richard Nixon advocated new towns in the 1968 presidential election campaign. A National Committee on Urban Growth Policy, formed by county officials, mayors, and congressional specialists on urban affairs, such as Representatives Thomas Ludlow Ashley (D., Ohio) and Henry Reuss (D., Wis.), and Senators John Sparkman (D., Ala.) and John Tower (R., Tx.), went all the way. The committee urged that the federal government help build no fewer than 100 new communities, averaging a population of 100,000 people each, adding them to ten new cities of at least one million inhabitants. Vice President Spiro Agnew signed the foreword to this proposal.

"The concept of the new city," Agnew's foreword said, "offers us a chance to discover what we really want from an urban environment and what we plan to bring to it." Good questions—and far from being answered.

This and other official recommendations stressed that a systematic policy of planning and building carefully sited new towns would contain urban sprawl and its catastrophic cost— the cost of ever more extended sewer lines, water mains, commuter highways, municipal services, and wasted energy, to say nothing of polluted land, water, and air. (It is mostly the suburban middle class that causes this drain on the national treasury, leaving little to pay for the needs of the poor who must stay in the city.)

The new towns policy statements said little about the cities and the poor. Yet the greatest promise of such a policy, properly conceived and carried out, is that it would provide a way out of the ghetto, and that it would restore the health of the old center cities.

In the context of resolute regional planning, racially and

economically integrated satellite communities can not only help arrest urban sprawl, but also provide housing, education, health care, and, most of all, jobs for people now wasting away in ghetto slums.

Bernard Weissbourd, a Chicago developer, and Herbert Channick, a lecturer in architecture, have proposed a national strategy to this effect. In a paper published by the Center for the Study of Democratic Institutions in September 1968, they urged:

"1) A massive ten-year program of development of new towns in outlying areas to accommodate the projected Negro and white population growth.

2) The construction in these towns of some additional 350,000 subsidized housing units each year for ten years, which will allow the ultimate replacement of urban substandard housing and create a temporary housing surplus.

3) The withdrawal of public expenditures for housing subsidies, sewer, water, roads, and mass transportation from ordinary subdivision development and their rechanneling into new towns, thus virtually eliminating the competition of segregated housing development."

The new town concept, Weissbourd and Channick argued, "lends itself admirably to dealing with the critical problems of our urban areas as well as with the race crisis."

The withdrawal of public expenditures from uncontrolled urban sprawl channels new development into desegregated and rationally ordered new communities and center city neighborhoods. It would put people and jobs together and thus increase employment opportunities and reduce commuting. It would permit the preservation of open country for recreation and the natural regeneration of air and water.

As to racial desegregation, Weissbourd and Channick present a convincing arithmetic, simplified to make their point:

"Assume that the population of a hypothetical metropolitan area is one million, of which 750,000 are white and 250,000 are Negro. If the Negroes are living in a ghetto and we want to desegregate and permit them to live anywhere, we should build

enough surplus housing units in outlying areas to accomodate a
fourth of this ghetto population and three times as many white
people. Thus, if we have

GHETTO	METROPOLITAN WHITE	OUTLYING AREA SURPLUS
250,000 N	750,000 W	250,000

and if we want to achieve the one-fourth, three-fourth
proportion in the population of the outlying area, the following
movements occur:

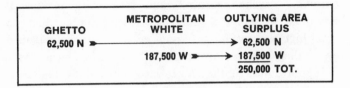

The vacancies resulting from the metropolitan white movement
to outlying areas makes possible a second movement of 187,000
Negroes from the ghetto into metropolitan white areas. The
result then is:

	GHETTO	METROPOLITAN WHITE	OUTLYING AREA SURPLUS
	250,000 N	750,000 W	
(1)	−62,500 N		62,500 N
(2)		−187,500 W	187,500 W
		562,500 W	
(3)	−187,500 N	187,500 N	
	0 N	750,000 TOT.	250,000 TOT.

The ghetto has been eliminated, and both the central city and
the surrounding metropolitan area are 25 percent black." The
key to this arithmetic is building a substantial housing surplus.

The Weissbourd-Channick chart illustrates a concept on which national urban policy ought to be based. The chart is much like the diagrams that illustrate Ebenezer Howard's proposal. Howard also left the actual design of garden cities to specific circumstances. Weissbourd offers an addendum to Howard's idea which, in my view, makes it not only a desirable, but also an essential path to real reform of urban America. It would use new towns as not only a means of achieving more rational land use and more pleasant living conditions, but it would also use new towns as a means of achieving a greater measure of social justice.

After 30 years and more of "slum clearance," "public housing," "urban renewal," and make-shift, make-work programs, we should have learned that gilding the ghetto (or other high concentrations of poor people) cannot eliminate or even reduce poverty. Poverty can only be reduced by increasing the opportunities for the poor to earn more money. There is no such opportunity in segregated concentrations of poor people—or the elderly, or any other minority group. Separate is inherently unequal.

Since Weissbourd published his proposal, there has been some migration of blacks from ghettos to suburbs, and—to a lesser extent—of whites from the suburbs to center cities. The percentage of blacks among the total number of people moving to the suburbs has not changed in the last 25 years, however. It is still only 5 percent.

Nor does it mean that a racial and economic balance and equal education and employment opportunities within the metropolitan region will come automatically. They will not—certainly not peacefully and within any time span our society can afford. Weissbourd's concerns and his proposed remedies are therefore just as valid and urgent now, as they were a decade ago when he published them while the ghettos were smoldering.

Although less talked about today, racial tension, center city decay, and urban sprawl are still formidable and disastrous. But they are not intractable. They will yield to determined policies.

Such policies must be realistic. It is not realistic, as Richard Nixon pointed out, to attempt what he called "forced integration of the suburbs." Unskilled and semiskilled blacks and Chicanos find little space to live, less employment, and much hostility in the suburbs. Efforts to compel wealthy dormitory suburbs to accept their "fair share" of subsidized housing have not found favor in the courts of law. The lily will not be tainted.

In planned communities, however, racial and economic integration has worked remarkably well.

Not that residents of Columbia or Reston are superior in tolerance and liberalism. But they willingly and often cheerfully accept people poorer and darker than themselves because they know that minorities will remain in the minority.

In a planned community, the privileged will not be overwhelmed or excluded by the underprivileged. Property values are not affected. School standards are not lowered by an overly large number of poorly educated children. The proportion—call it "the quota," if you will—which the majority deems acceptable is fixed in the new town masterplan.

The masterplan assures stability. It makes sure that subsidized housing is built in small clusters throughout the community. Ghettos and a high number of underprivileged students in any one school are thus avoided. The streets and yards of the poor are more readily kept as clean as those of the rich. Garbage is picked up by the same trucks. Both groups share playgrounds and community centers.

There was once or twice an open outbreak of tension between black and white residents of Reston. But this, as everyone concerned admitted, was because the masterplan principle was not well observed. Two subsidized Reston housing projects were designed to be too large, placed out of the way, and therefore often neglected.

At first, blacks seemed to welcome the new town concept. New towns are "the black man's hope" wrote Edward G. Sharp, a black resident of Reston, who saw no hope in the center city ghetto.

Then, for a while, in the wake of the riots, the notion of "black power" took hold of the civil rights movement and black power was understood to mean black concentration and black separatism.

The "black power" idea was invented by two white sociologists, Frances Piven and Richard Cloward of the Columbia University School of Social Work. It proved to be fallacious. Black power does not depend on real estate. Whether a precinct, ward, or district is entirely or only partially black does not affect the number of representatives it can elect, or the influence these representatives wield in city hall, state legislature, or Congress. On the contrary, geographic distribution is more likely to increase political consideration of black interests than black concentration.

At any rate, the separatist phase in black political strategy was short-lived, and while few black leaders hail new towns as "the black man's hope," none have voiced opposition. There are too few new towns for them to think about, one way or another. It is well established, however, that most people in the ghetto would move out if they could, and it is reasonable to assume that blacks would support the Weissbourd concept if government were to consider it seriously.

It never did—not really.

President Johnson and his advisors, notably Richard Goodwin, grasped the enormous potential of the idea. But the Johnson administration bungled it, and the Nixon-Ford administrations did the discrediting.

20 Test in a Hurricane

New communities, "freshly planned and built," deserve the encouragement and support of the federal government, Johnson told Congress in his message on housing and cities in February 1968. "We have already seen their birth," he added. "Here in the nation's capital, on surplus land once owned by the government, a new community is springing up." It never sprang, however. The great experiment that was to be Lyndon Johnson's farewell gift to the nation was not really born. It was stillborn.

The conception of Fort Lincoln, as the town was to be called, was exhilarating. It started with a suggestion by sociologist Harvey Perloff that if new towns out in the country are a good idea, why not build "new towns—in town" on large vacant sites in the city? This was followed by an open letter to President Johnson in *The Washington Post,* suggesting that the site of the departing National Training School for Boys at the northeast gateway to Washington, D.C., was ideal for a national demonstration of the concept. (The Training School, a euphemism for a federal prison for juvenile delinquents, was moving to West Virginia.)

It took the White House almost two years to ponder the suggestion, but then President Johnson wanted action in a hurry.

HUD, on a day's notice, summoned Moshe Safdie, Paul

Rudolph, and other leading architects to Washington to produce innovative and economical building designs. The city's local building code bureaucrats rejected them all.

Citizens living near the Fort Lincoln site tied the entire project into knots for months, quarreling about citizen participation in the planning of a town that was not to have any citizens for years to come.

The local urban renewal agency, known as the Redevelopment Land Agency, hurriedly built some housing for the elderly and a school on the site, only to satisfy White House demands for quick action. The housing is terrible and the school stood empty for years because the elderly don't have school children.

After these and many other grotesque shenanigans, Mayor Walter Washington commissioned a team, headed by Edward J. Logue, to produce a plan. Logue later headed the New York State Urban Development Corporation.

It was a dandy plan. Unlike most city plans, it resembled neither a Mondrian painting, nor a still life of potato sacks in diverse colors, denoting the kind of zoning proposed. Neither did it show a country club community. It showed a compact, urban place.

The plan focused on the workings of the proposed town, the human interaction, the life to be led there. It was to be a multiclass community going first class. It was to offer livability.

Foremost among the special features of Logue's Fort Lincoln plan were exceptionally good schools and a monorail to replace automobiles.

The superior schools, administered by a separate educational institution free of Washington's stifling school board bureaucracy, were to induce upper-and middle-income families to live alongside low-income families.

The monorail was to free space usually devoted to wide motor roads and parking, thus achieving high density amid greenery and clean air. The Logue plan called for housing for 4,500 families plus shopping, recreation, schools, a college, some industry, and much lively bustle on 335 acres.

What toppled the plan was precisely that which made it so

convincing. It was designed, as a good community must be designed, as one intricate structure in which each part is dependent on the others, like a house of cards.

Take away the special schools, and hopes for attracting affluent families will vanish. Take away the monorail, and there will have to be expensive motor roads and parking lots, and far less lucrative space for people. And so it went. A bureaucracy, flabbergasted by the boldness of the plan, poked at card after card until the whole structure collapsed.

No one—not Johnson with his White House, Robert Weaver with his Department of Housing and Urban Development, Mayor Walter Washington with city hall, none of the planners who made their living deploring the urban crisis, no architect extolling the virtues of noble planning, no citizen concerned for civic amenity—no one uttered so much as a murmur in defense of what they all would have been so boastfully proud had it succeeded without effort.

The project sank into the morass of Washington's bureaucracy. Its only trace is a desultory hovel of mediocre suburban builders' homes.

Logue took his plans back to New York City where his main ideas are now incorporated in Roosevelt Island, the new town in the East River built by the New York State Development Corporation. It is only partly completed at this time, but already, in the eyes of most residents, a full success.

Richard Nixon's 1970 State of the Union message picked up where Johnson left off, calling for planned urban growth. He added that "the federal government must be in a position to assist in the building of new cities and the rebuilding of old ones."

From October 1969, in fact, Nixon's Department of Housing and Urban Development, headed by a bewildered George Romney, had an enthusiastic lawyer, William Nicoson, working on the idea of assisting new cities.

"I am with you," Nicoson was told by President Nixon's assistant, Daniel Patrick Moynihan, who had also been prominent in the Kennedy administration. "We are setting up an interdepartmental task force to study proposals for new legislation."

"By November," Nicoson recalled later in an article contained in an anthology on *New Perspectives on Community Development,* "Moynihan was clearly not with us, but unfortunately his interdepartmental task force was."

In no time at all, Nixon's announced policy had been crushed in the rivalry between Nixon's policy advisors—Moynihan and John Ehrlichman.

Each, as Nicoson tells it, "sought initially to stake a paternity claim for any new initiatives that might eventually emerge. The rivalry ended with the 'promotion' of Moynihan to the post of 'Counsellor,' effectively severing him from the policy-making machinery (the staff of the Urban and Rural Affairs Council, later the Domestic Council) over which Ehrlichman took command. As soon as this outcome became evident within the White House, Daniel Moynihan lost all interest in new community initiatives and actively encouraged the attendance of the principal academic opponent of the new community concept at several government meetings. Ehrlichman, on the other hand, became too busy with the crisis-management aspects of his new responsibilities to devote much time to new community initiatives . . ."

All was confusion, and, according to Nicoson, led to nothing more than endless rounds of interdepartmental task-force staff meetings in which objections were exchanged and nothing was decided.

Instead, Congress took the initiative. Representative Ashley circulated a draft bill calling for a massive $22 billion, five-year program of federal grants and loans for new town development. Suddenly, Ehrlichman got interested in the program. He could not, after all, allow a Democratic Congress to seem more enterprising than the Republican White House. The game was now played by different players. It was no longer Moynihan versus Ehrlichman, but White House versus Congress.

The next move was Ashley's. As soon as he heard that Ehrlichman had called a meeting of the White House Urban

Affairs Council for March 26, 1970, Ashley, together with Senator Sparkman, rushed to place their draft bill on the congressional agenda. They made it on March 25, but lost the $22 billion in their haste. To get agreement all around, the authorization figures had to be left blank. That proved fatal.

The congressmen needn't have rushed. Ehrlichman's council meeting, as usual, decided nothing.

Nicoson's article tries to convey the flavor of the discussion that followed his presentation of the HUD proposal. "While the dialogue is grossly simplified," he writes, "it reflects general positions taken by the participants, to the best of my five-year recollection:

Robert Finch (secretary of Health, Education and Welfare): Don't you have examples of poor urban development outside California?

Spiro Agnew (vice president, presiding in the absence of the president): We need to put new cities way out there far from existing cities.

John Volpe (secretary of Transportation): We need to improve existing cities, particularly existing transportation.

Paul McCracken (chairman of the Council of Economic Advisers): I would not favor any initiative that flies in the face of the free market. Let the market determine where the growth occurs.

George Shultz (secretary of Labor; shortly to become director of the Office of Management and Budget): You are proposing new categorical grants, but the administration backs revenue sharing.

John Ehrlichman (executive secretary of the council): From my Seattle law practice experience, I wonder whether we know how to build new communities. (Exits to take a phone call.)

Donald Rumsfeld (director of the Office of Economic Opportunity): There will be growth on the periphery of cities whatever we do. Why shouldn't we try to improve its quality?

Spiro Agnew: We need to put new cities way out there far from existing cities.

George Romney (HUD secretary): We are milling around in

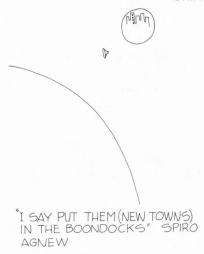

"I SAY PUT THEM (NEW TOWNS)
IN THE BOONDOCKS" SPIRO
AGNEW

this meeting! We can decide later where to put new communities. The issue to be decided today is whether to offer more assistance in putting them *somewhere*.

Spiro Agnew: Columbia was a pain in the neck while I was governor (of Maryland). I say put them in the boondocks.

John Ehrlichman (returning from another phone call): We'll continue this later. I have to fly to San Clemente."

Nicoson adds: "While present for only portions of the discussion, John Ehrlichman had been able to observe himself the results of interdepartmental consultation. The meeting was never continued."

Instead, Romney and Ehrlichman agreed that further council discussion was hopeless and that a memorandum with HUD's proposals for new community legislation should be immediately submitted to the president. As was customary, the memorandum would appear to transmit recommendations from the council. Ehrlichman also insisted that it be ready for the next day's afternoon courier to San Clemente. Memoranda to Nixon had to be written in sets of tersely stated options, with a place at each option for the president to check his preference. Policy arguments for or against each option had to be stated in a brief sentence or two. There was to be no exposition of the issues. Ehrlichman's staff further desiccated this score card.

Two months later, Nicoson was told that the score was zero. Nixon refused to check any of the options because new spending would increase inflationary pressures. Nicoson argued that, on the contrary, planned communities save capital expenditures for land, streets, sewers and water mains. He could not persuade his boss, George Romney, to take this argument to the White House. Romney knew that Nixon felt safer checking secluded paper options than discussing decisions face-to-face with his cabinet members.

Meanwhile, Congress passed legislation calling for a national urban growth policy (to be spelled out in a biannual White House report), and a loan and grants program to encourage private developers to build comprehensively planned and economically integrated new communities. This legislation is known as Title VII of the 1970 Housing and Urban Development Act. It was signed by Nixon on December 31, 1970.

Nicoson suspects that the president was never told just what Title VII contained. The White House staff and the Office of Management and Budget, at any rate, did their best to ignore and sabotage it. After two years of frustration, Nicoson resigned.

Early in 1975, *The Washington Post* ran a lyrical photograph of Reston's Lake Anne Village Center five days in a row. It served as a logo for a series of five articles entitled "New Towns: A Fading Dream." The articles reported, without comprehending subtlety, that of the 15 new towns projects receiving federal Title VII assistance, 15 were either bankrupt or close to bankruptcy. From this they deduced that new towns are a costly failure.

The Reston picture was outright unfair because neither Reston—nor Columbia, for that matter—had participated in the Title VII program. Both the Gulf-Reston Corporation managers and James Rouse considered the half-hearted federal attempt not an aid but a hindrance. The *Post* articles also never mentioned that it was the government that had failed, not the new towns.

Lengthy study reports have been written explaining how and

why the 15 government-assisted new towns floundered. But the reasons can be summed up as follows: Title VII, as finally written, was not only legalistically confusing, it was also based on a fundamental misconception that defeated its purpose. The second reason should be obvious from the first: the Nixon administration did not want the new towns program to work.

The legislative misconception surrounding the program was that any private developer could build a new town anywhere, all by himself, provided he met a set of government requirements and was given financial assistance to tide him over until the roads and sewers were in, the first houses built, and the cash started flowing.

That is nonsense. No private developer can build a whole new town without the active support of state and local governments.

In the first place, there is no point in building the new town unless it can thrive and help assure urban order. That is only possible in the right location—right, that is, in terms of where people want to live in relation to their jobs, their cultural opportunities, and their recreation; and, where the public interest demands that they live in relation to public transportation, the sewer, water, and electric network, and sound environmental and energy planning. A private developer will rarely, if ever, obtain a site that meets these requirements. It only happened once—at Columbia—and Rouse, who brought it off, assures everyone who cares to know that it is not likely ever to happen again. Only government with its resources and its power of eminent domain is able to acquire the land for the town, including land for recreation and a protective greenbelt.

Second, building a town, or even a small planned and integrated community, requires zoning changes, access roads and rails, schools, hospitals, police and fire protection, inducements for industry to move in, housing subsidies for the low-income families who must be included, and a host of other things that only government can provide. Building a town involves all levels of government—federal, state, and local.

This does not mean, however, that the three levels of government and their bureaucrats should attempt the job directly. The best way to do it, in the almost unanimous opinion of everyone who has seriously looked into the matter, is with a fresh, new, public and nonprofit development corporation invested with governmental powers; that is, the power of eminent domain, the power to raise bonds, and the power to override local zoning and building codes. We have such a corporation in this country and it has been doing very well—the New York State Urban Development Corporation, established in 1968 under Governor Nelson Rockefeller.

The New York State legislature voted for the corporation in a hastily summoned session within hours of Dr. Martin Luther King's assassination, while the ghettos started to burn. Originally headed by Logue, who conceived the development corporation idea and had been in charge of the urban renewal in New Haven and Boston, it still functions well, building new communities, housing, and public buildings all over the state of New York.

So far, other states have not followed the example because, despite its flawless record, the New York State UDC acquired a bad reputation—as tragically undeserved as the reputation of the new town idea.

New York's UDC was the first institution to get involved in New York's financial crisis. Logue and his corporation were noisily charged with excessive spending and borrowing. What happened, as a stern commission of bankers found after an exhaustive investigation, was that UDC could not increase its income as fast as it had to increase its expenditures.

The reasons income fell behind were inflation, recession, and President Nixon's moratorium on federal housing subsidies. Inflation increased construction and maintenance costs. The recession slowed the sale and rental of new buildings. And the Nixon moratorium stopped promised federal subsidy payments.

There was no way for the corporation to increase rents as fast as it had to increase expenditures. There was also no way for the corporation to curb expenditures because a half-completed housing project is a lot more expensive than the additional unforeseen cost of completing it. On the contrary, UDC had to rush completion so its buildings could start making money and keep the cash flow moving. But rushing completion meant borrowing more money.

The investigating bankers acknowledged that in time UDC would have been capable of repaying its debts and interest charges and that its investments were sound. After some stoppages and reductions in its ambitious program, UDC resumed its operation. But the publicity about its financial difficulties, created mostly by the bankers' sudden refusal to lend, scared Congress and state legislatures away from the idea.

The same happened essentially to the 15 new towns. There was no way under the circumstances for a private new town *not* to go bankrupt. Title VII required developers to include subsidized housing, but under the moratorium the subsidies did not come forth. This meant that the developers could not build homes for the people for whom they had already built shops and roads. In addition, there was no moratorium on the real estate taxes and on the interest they had to pay on their mortgage loans. What is more, the Nixon administration impounded some of the funds earmarked for new communities. Local highway departments broke promises. Local zoning and planning commissions fussed and fussed. But the federal Department of Housing and Urban Development did little or nothing to help, if only to protect its own investments. As we have seen, the Nixon administration decided to sabotage the program.

"Launching a new towns program in the early 1970s was like asking the Wright Brothers to test their airplane in a hurricane and then concluding, when it crashed, that the invention did not work," observed Michael Spear, Columbia's general manager.

Carla Hills, who became secretary of Housing and Urban Development under President Ford, believed in the invention, but came too late with her perceptive intelligence to make it fly. Patricia Harris, who succeeded her under President Carter, could do nothing more than suspend further federal loan guarantees for new community development.

So here, too, it is back to the drawing board.

What must be designed, first of all, are new ways of informing the American people about the need for orderly and socially just urban development and redevelopment programs. In large part it is a matter of politics, literally, because *polis* is Greek for city.

Americans are no longer frightened that planning will bring about regimentation. We all see that in the suburbs or the ghetto, it is nonplanning that limits our choices and our freedom to live as we please without fear. What scares Americans about national planning, regional planning, and planned communities is the fear that the government will bungle it and that it will cost a lot of money.

The former is a matter of citizen participation and education, of careful public control. It is not easy. As to cost, it is far less expensive to build a good environment than a bad one.

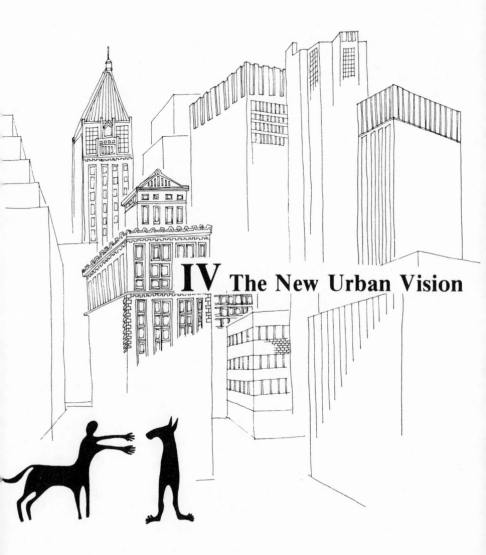

IV The New Urban Vision

21 Seven Precepts

The new mood was at first mostly negative, much like the rebellious mind that gave rise to abstract architecture in the 1920s in Europe. It rejected technocracy and "plastic," mass-produced monotony, the bulldozing of nice old buildings, fast-food chains, glass boxes, urban renewal, freeways, and, of course, pollution and wasted energy.

But lately, I sense that a positive, new urban vision is beginning to emerge. It is not as radical a departure from the vision of the past 50 years as was abstract architecture from *Beaux Arts*, and *La Ville Radieuse* from "the City Beautiful." It builds on the new town movement, rather than the Modern movement; on the ideas of Ebenezer Howard, rather than those of Le Corbusier. But Howard's ideas are as much of our time as those of Le Corbusier. The difference is basic, however: Howard is concerned with people and their relation to nature. Le Corbusier is concerned with art and its relation to technology. The Garden City is a social, democratic concept. The Radiant City is an intellectual, elitist concept. And we are heading toward social, popular, and democratic architectural and environmental design.

The new urban vision I see is based on seven precepts. (Seven seems to be a magic number in design philosophy. Remember John Ruskin's *Seven Lamps of Architecture*?) My precepts are not original. They have developed in many minds along with the new mood. And though you may find one or two of them set forth elsewhere, or even in practice here or there, they are primarily articles of faith. But they seem to me a faith worth forging into a program for citizens to support and take to their planners, their zoning boards, and their politicians—with the demand that they be adopted as policy:

1) The city is here to stay. Strong center cities have always been, and will continue to be, the center of civilization. We should not suburbanize the city, nor urbanize the suburbs. "Downtown" should not be a mere "central business district," but a delightful cultural, educational, and recreational experience for everyone.

2) A good place to live is inclusive, not exclusive and segregated. We must reintegrate our disintegrating habitat, enlarge its choices, opportunities, and benefits for everyone, thus making it more democratic.

3) Mobility is nice, but stability is nicer. Our preoccupation with spinning our wheels faster, with transportation and traffic, must yield to locating the essentials of life in close proximity. We need greater emphasis on antitransportation planning rather than transportation planning. We must stop thinking of transportation only in terms of private automobiles, subways, and buses, and start thinking of a whole array of vehicles, including the good old trolley and taxi, augmenting each other in a transportation *system* that moves like clockwork.

4) The problems of the city and the suburbs cannot be solved within the city limits and suburban jurisdictions. We must think, plan, and act on a regional scale.

5) While we can solve urban problems only in the context of urban regions, or metropolitan areas, we live—and ought to solve our human problems—in neighborhoods. Only our neighborhood can give us a sense of belonging. Neighborhoods are the foundation stones on which cities, suburbs, and metropolitan areas are built. They must be the basis of urban planning and the focus of our attention.

6) The effort to accomodate the city to the machine age has failed. The results of modern city planning are neither efficient

nor satisfying. Economic efficiency and the human need for identity and historic continuity demand urban conservation rather than urban renewal, and the preservation and adoption of old buildings to new uses rather than their replacement.

7) Our psychological need for more lovable and more livable surroundings and our practical need to conserve energy cry out for a more human, representational rather than abstract architecture. We must learn to design our buildings and communities *with* nature, not in defiance of nature. The new architecture seems to be on its way.

And so is all of the above. The new urban vision is not visionary. It is beginning to come into focus.

22 The Best Economy

"The question which now interests people is, what are we going to do with democracy now that we have it? What kind of society are we going to make by its aid? Are we to see nothing but an endless vista of Londons and Manchesters, New Yorks and Chicagos, with their noise and ugliness, their money-getting, their 'corners' and 'rings,' their strikes, their contrasts of luxury and squalor? Or shall we be able to build a society with art and culture for all, and with some great spiritual aim dominating men's lives?"

The question was asked on March 5, 1891, by an editorial writer of the London *Daily Chronicle*. It is quoted in Sir Ebenezer Howard's little book.

A first impulse is to answer no. Democracy has not been able to create better cities, or build a society with art and culture for all. Cities have become worse in the nearly hundred years since the question was asked. I am sure, at any rate, that this is what most Americans believe. Even some urban experts assert—or did just a few years ago—that cities are obsolete and doomed.

This is utter nonsense, of course. Even the horrors of World War II could not doom Warsaw, Rotterdam, Coventry, Berlin, Stalingrad, or Hiroshima for long. They became thriving, bustling, traffic-jammed phoenixes within a decade or so. San Francisco survived not only the earthquake of 1906, but the experts who warned San Franciscans not to entertain any serious hopes for the future of their city. Even as these soothsayers spoke, even before the ground had cooled, residents started shoveling and hammering. Nine years later, San Francisco held a dazzling world's fair.

Whether you believe their future glum or bright, there is no alternative to cities. It will be expensive, to be sure, to catch up with a century of stagnation. While we have made amazing progress in the efficiency of gourmet kitchen machines and push-button dishwashers, we have made no progress whatsoever in disposing of potato peels and dishwater after they leave the kitchen. There has been no really useful invention to make cities work better since the sewer pipe and treatment plant and the fire hydrant—and these few improvements have been allowed to deteriorate.

The replacement of 1,500 miles of dangerously antiquated sewers in New York City alone will cost about $310 million a year for over 20 years. Boston is losing half its fresh water through leaky pipes at a cost of $7 million a year. It will take untold billions of dollars to update the antiquated network of underground pipes, cables, tunnels, and manholes in sufficiently safe condition to support our increasingly mechanized society for another hundred years, say recent government sponsored studies.

But it would be immeasurably more costly—it would simply not be possible—to abandon cities. How would you do it? Benignly neglected sores on our body politic would be highly contagious. And suppose we could let the old central cities die, how would we dispose of the corpse? Nuclear cremation?

To live, however, cities must be lively. To pay for the billions needed for sewer repair, they must invest in livability, amenity, and, yes, luxury. Inducements for such things as sidewalk cafes and a pleasant plaza, subsidies for such things as concert halls, public swimming pools, and amusement and recreation parks, are essential downpayments on the large sums required for the essential sanitation of sewers and slums.

And while it is seldom clearly said that attractive cities are as vital to the nation's health and welfare as adequate defense and

orderly commerce, it is, I believe, increasingly understood—
and acted upon. That, too, is part of the new mood.

If we rise above the sludge of facile clichés about urban doom
and crisis and really look at what is happening to the cities, we
see a great deal that is good and encouraging. The endless vista
of the industrial, coal-blackened city the *Daily Chronicle* had in
mind has changed considerably. And despite large slum areas,
acres of abandoned buildings, freeways, and isolated glass
boxes, the city has changed for the better.

The most important change in America is a change of mind. I
remember when, in 1962, the first sidewalk cafe in Washington,
Bassin's, applied for its license at Fourteenth Street and
Pennsylvania Avenue. There was an excited hearing. The
health department testified that eating outdoors would poison
us. The Daughters of the American Revolution asserted that
sidewalk cafes would encourage prostitution and other wicked
things. The traffic engineers complained that the cafe would
impede traffic. I cheered Bassin's on in *The Washington Post*,
but my managing editor at the time, Alfred Friendly, tried to

curb my enthusiasm. "This European stuff will never go in America."

Friendly moved to Europe, and Washington now has about 100 sidewalk cafes. There are 300 in Manhattan, and the New York Planning Department is encouraging more.

And, yes, we *are* building a society with art and culture. There must have been at least 100 new museums and cultural centers built in the past decade or two in as many American cities. The funds seeded by the National Endowment for the Arts have brought forth an unprecedented flowering. The Endowment's Architecture and Environment program has, with small amounts of money, stimulated a large amount of creative city thinking—such as remodeling old railroad stations into arts centers or restaurants, making use of rooftops for playgrounds, sunbathing and victory gardens, and painting cheerful murals on drab fire walls.

It is this kind of thinking and doing, the little things, rather than massive infusions of money alone, that promise to make our cities more livable.

An example is Seattle during its depression in 1970. The Boeing Corporation, the area's largest employer, had laid off more than 50,000 people. Engineers delivered drycleaning. Computer programmers drove cabs. Skilled tool and dye makers began making jewelry in their basements. People who had been caught up in their jobs, who could never find time for culture, suddenly had lots of time but very little money. They discovered parks, libraries, and museums, and Mayor Wes Uhlman launched an extensive arts program.

Despite the depression, Mayor Uhlman invested half a million dollars of city funds a year to support local theater, dance, and music groups; to purchase concert tickets for young and old citizens; and to help struggling arts organizations to survive. The funds were soon matched by the National Endowment for the Arts.

This didn't put butter on the parsnips of the unemployed, but it was a great boost to morale. It at least eased the mental depression.

"The lesson learned in Seattle," Uhlman reported later, "is

that we all must begin to view the arts not as a luxury for the elite but rather as a basic city service like police, fire protection, garbage collection, or street paving, and that if we support our artists and treat them with respect, they respond by enriching our city and the life of virtually every citizen . . . If art reflects and prefigures the changing human condition then the artist is indispensible to us if we are to survive the future with our humanism intact."

"The city has undergone many changes during the last 5,000 years," Lewis Mumford wrote, "and further changes are doubtless in store. But the innovations that beckon, urgently, are not in the extension and perfection of physical equipment; still less in multiplying automatic electronic devices for dispersing into formless suburban dust the remaining organs of culture. Just the contrary: significant improvements will come only through applying art and through the city's central human concerns, with a fresh dedication to the cosmic and ecological processes that enfold all beings. We must restore the city to the maternal, life-nuturing functions, the autonomous activities, the symbiotic associations that have long been neglected or suppressed. For the city should be an organ of love; and the best economy of cities is the care and culture of men."

Modern city planning and abstract architecture have never understood that. They still don't.

23 Renaissance and Risorgimento

If Detroit ever has a renaissance—and God knows it needs one—it will happen despite its flashy, new Renaissance Center. Completed in 1977, the skyscraping bundle of glass tubes on the Detroit River is really a counter-Renaissance Center. It is at best an example of modern city planning's exclusive reliance on the "perfection of physical equipment," as Mumford called it, without regard for the intricacy of the urban fabric. It cuts the city off from its river as effectively as the nineteenth-century industrial plants and warehouses. And, in keeping with Le Corbusier's and CIAM's misguided notions, it concentrates and segregates one vital urban function—high-style commerce and tourism—from the rest of the city's life to the detriment of both.

At the time the Detroit Renaissance Center was built, New York City planners began the revitalization of a frisky, but declining (mostly lower middle-class) neighborhood in an altogether different spirit with altogether different methods. The *risorgimento* of Little Italy, which is roughly between Greenwich Village and Chinatown in Lower Manhattan, is hardly comparable in terms of expenditure and scale with what was done in Detroit. But it illustrates a new approach to the rejuvenation of declining cities, an approach that preserves and strengthens the integration of a variety of people and activities that make neighborhoods and cities lively.

RenCen, as Detroiters call it, consists of a 73-story, 1,400-room hotel; meeting rooms and halls for large conventions; four office towers with 2.2 million square feet of rentable space; parking for 6,000 cars; and a carnival of four movie theaters, 13 restaurants, a suburban shopping-center worth of shops, cocktail lounges, splashing water, greenery, glitter, and Muzak-drenched confusion.

All this obviously draws business, people, and vitality from Detroit's already decaying downtown, six or seven blocks away. Once you have entered RenCen, there is no reason to leave it again until it is time to go home or your money runs out.

But entering the glass towers is extremely difficult if you attempt it on foot. My excuse for being so maladroit in Detroit is that before my visit, I had dinner nearby with a friend and there weren't any taxis. So, with much apprehension (Detroit has one of the highest crime rates), I negotiated several deserted and partly abandoned blocks of urban no-man's land until I came to a formidable barrier—ten-lane Jefferson Avenue, a nasty highway that clearly was not designed to be crossed by anything.

A pedestrian must pass two more tests before he may be admitted to architect John Portman's never-never megastructure. First, he must prove his courage by walking the driveway through a forbidding "berm," a concrete rampart that looks suspiciously like a Berlin Wall erected to keep the natives out, but built, I am told, to house heating and airconditioning machinery. Next, he must prove his ingenuity by finding his way through a labyrinth of driveways, without signs or sidewalks, until he finds the all but hidden entrance into drive-in Portman-land.

The reward is that, once inside, you may plunk into any one of a myriad of cushiony seats on any of six levels—by the pond, under a waterfall, perching on a daringly cantilevered "cocktail pod"—looking up into dangling greenery or down on teeming humanity—and that at the flash of your credit card, an apparition will appear on a motorized refreshment wagon and sell you a drink.

The scene is at once lively and monotonous. You are inside the huge platform from which all the glass tubes sprout. It is an enormous, exciting space, filled with giant concrete columns that support the skyscrapers above, as well as elevator shafts, a multitude of escalators, spiral staircases that mesh the various levels and galleries and pods and ends. Portman is famous for these grand, somewhat adrenalized courts. He used them at the Peachtree Center in Atlanta, and the Embarcadero Center in San Francisco.

The space is monotonous once you walk around. In Detroit, the combined hotel lobby and shopping mall form a circle. You walk around and around expecting some surprise, but it is always the same. You get dizzy and confused. I never quite knew where I was. The poor graphics did not help. Different shops and window displays might have helped. But at the time of my visit in the spring of 1978, few shops had opened, although the offices were renting well and conventions were booked for years.

RenCen is touted as one of the largest privately financed urban developments in the nation's history. It was launched on the initiative of Henry Ford II for the often expressed purpose of helping Detroit out of its despair, of showing confidence in the city. By the time it was finished, it showed over half a billion dollars worth of confidence. Ford was joined by 50 other corporations.

Wayne Doran, the amiable and frank spokesman for these investors, says the demonstration of confidence is as much psychological as physical. Psychologically, it may indeed have accelerated plans for other skyscrapers and shopping centers in downtown Detroit, and a federally assisted "people mover" system, linking the central business district with the cultural center—the Art Institute, the library, and Wayne State University with its various institutions—further up Woodward Avenue. Psychologically, it is also true, no doubt, that the sight of the gleaming glass tubes makes many a Detroit heart beat faster, although the more impressive view of this fortress is from the Canadian side of the river.

But while Mayor Coleman Young is loudly and frequently praising RenCen, I heard much bitter talk about it on the part of Detroit housing and planning officials. Some see it as a capitalist plot against the city. The bitterness is understandable if you travel about in what one writer has called "the city of urban despair." Block after block of abandoned, looted, and burned cottages on weedy, littered plots look even more depressing than abandoned, looted, and burned-out tenements in Brooklyn. The shocking sight is one occupied house, in a sea of dead ones, with a horde of children playing in the debris of a broken-down porch.

RenCen does nothing for these children and Doran says irrefutably that it never promised to solve the city's social problems. It provides 3,000 jobs, he says, and is bringing thousands of conventioneers into the city. The trouble is, few of them venture across Jefferson Avenue.

The city, together with RenCen, will have to spend thought and money on building links to downtown, if the half billion dollar investment is to stop hurting Detroit and start helping. Well-lit greenways and walkways and minibus service to the restaurants and boutiques of Greektown and other attractions are imperative. The sooner that silly "berm" is buried, the better.

I am sure the deplorable insularity of RenCen is not due to ill will, as some people charge, but to the naivete of American business in matters of city planning and architecture. The riverfront site was easily available (although the city planners wanted it turned into a park). There was no need, as Doran pointed out, to displace anyone. It had a good view. Nor could Ford and his partners conceive of a manifestation of power and confidence that did not scrape the sky. Even Paris and London have succumbed to the Promethean temptation.

But just think what Henry Ford II and his 50 partners might have accomplished for Detroit if they had laid their half-billion dollar towers on end. It would have yielded at least 12-square blocks of new buildings—plazas, covered malls, greenery, splashing water, glitter, Muzak-drenched confusion, motorized barmaids, and all.

In Manhattan, Little Italy's revitalization and a whole reorientation of New York City's approach to community development is the work of the city's Urban Design Group, a sort of architectural task force of the City Planning Commission, established in 1972 by Mayor John Lindsay on the recommendation of architect Philip Johnson. The group was to give New York's routine planning that extra creative quality that is so often dismissed as mere aesthetic frill, but can make the difference between success and failure of a project.

The first head of the Urban Design Group was an architect of the "make no-little-plans" school who, given half a chance, would have plunked a 12-cylinder RenCen in the middle of SoHo's remodeled cast-iron lofts. He was succeeded by an Israeli architect-planner, Raquel Ramati, who believes in the fine-grain details of planning. For old neighborhoods and new

skyscrapers alike, Ramati and her team try to find the
ingredients of healthy and pleasant city life so they can
strengthen or create them. It doesn't cost the city any money,
because it is done with zoning and building regulations, and the
bonuses a city can give a builder in return for public favors: We
will give you five stories of rentable office space above what the
zoning permits, if you give us a sunken shopping plaza, a row of
trees and a fountain. It is the new urban game and everybody
wins. The city wins its plaza and the builder wins a profit from
the extra space. With its bonuses, a smart city planning office
can obtain amenities—open space, small parks, benches, public
art—for which the city council could never find the funds.

In Little Italy, the Urban Design Group worked with a local
citizen organization, the Little Italy Restoration Association,
or LIRA, to define what precisely gives the neighborhood its
special charm, ambience, and flavor. It then set down these
characteristics in special legislation that is in part quite unusual.
(The special legislation was possible because the area had been
declared a Special Zoning District.) For instance, Little Italy's
old tenements, built before the housing reforms of the 1930s,
are set flush with the lot line, using every inch of space. The
reformed building codes would not permit that. It was not
considered "decent, safe, and sanitary," as worded by the law.
The reforms insisted on setbacks, which brought mangy lawns,
much litter, and high-rise buildings. That destroyed the
character, charm, and ambience of Little Italy.

Ramati's special zoning allowed the unreformed type of
building again, taking care of decency, safety, and sanitation in
other ways. Ramati undid the errors of modern planning
theories, in effect, and restored the integrity of the street. She
made rules requiring new buildings to harmonize with the old,
not only in height, but also in use of building materials. She
required street-level shops, as in the old days, with window sills
on their store front, and signs in the old dimensions. Parks were
sorely needed, and large developers in the area were given
special bonuses in return for building or improving open space.

One would expect the developers to curse all these special

regulations as bureaucratic chicanery, and take their construction cranes to the suburbs where anything goes. Not so.

The design controls assure builders and investors that Little Italy will remain Little Italy, *pasta, prosciutto,* street festivals, bunting, and *mamma mia.* A stable neighborhood with a stable character is a good investment.

24 Hearing the Fountains Play

The antifreeway protests of the 1960s, the thickening pollution over our cities, and the scarcity and rising cost of oil, have finally curbed the arrogant power of the highway lobby. Early in 1978, the Carter administration's Department of Transportation proposed legislation that would give public transportation as much federal assistance as freeways. It would give state and local officials more authority to decide how best to meet their transportation needs. (In the past it was usually an eight-lane freeway or nothing). It would insist on a single transportation plan in which all modes of moving people are given equal consideration.

Perhaps the tyranny of the private automobile is at last coming to an end. According to the calculations of sociologist Ivan Illich, this tyranny costs the average American 1,500 hours a year (that's 187½ working days, or 37½ work weeks) driving, parking, and earning the keep of a car.

A good omen that we may indeed have stopped strangling our cities in freeways is to be found in what sculptor-designer Angela Danadjieva described as putting "a green lid over the whole disaster." The "whole disaster" is Seattle's Interstate Highway I-5, ten sunken lanes of concrete, speeding an average of 133,290 noisy motor vehicles into and through Seattle's city center each day. A steaming canyon, torn across the city by an earthquake, could not have been worse. Under Mayor Uhlman,

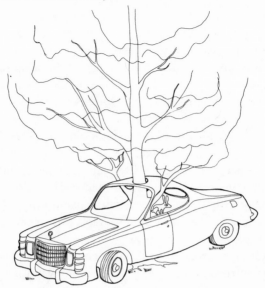

the city finally decided what had to be done. They covered the canyon with a park.

The "green lid" is the work of landscape architects Lawrence Halprin and Associates, with Angela Danadjieva, a recent immigrant from Bulgaria, as the leading designer. It is an enchantment and displays the kind of grandeur usually associated with natural wonders. It encompasses many moods. It balances motion and stillness. There are roaring "water curtains," grassy amphitheaters, quiet sitting areas, and marvelous views over one of the most beautiful cities in this country. Seattle's freeway cover is not as large as New York's Central Park, but it is of the same civic importance. Besides, its greenery hides an eyesore and its many water fountains baffle the noise of the combustion engines. In time, I am sure, more freeway ditches and spaghetti will be hidden or removed, just as we are clearing our waterfronts of the ugly flotsam of coal-powered industry.

And as we put the automobile in its place, we are discovering the delights—and commercial value—of returning streets to people. Our love affair with the automobile made us slow learners in this respect. The great American landscape and urban designer Frederick Law Olmsted realized more than a century ago that in the interest of mutual convenience, pedestrian and vehicular traffic ought to be separated. This principle is handsomely observed in New York's Central Park, which Olmsted designed with architect Calvert Vaux in 1857.

Clarence Stein, as we have seen, extended this principle to residential precincts in his design for Radburn in 1929. The idea of reserving the town agora, the central meeting and market place, for people on foot, was first realized in the reconstruction of Rotterdam and Coventry, immediately after World War II. Beginning with Stevenage, which was planned in 1946, a car-free town center became one of the most prominent characteristics of the British new towns.

Victor Gruen, one of the leading city planners of our time, tried to introduce the idea in America in 1956 with his Fort Worth plan. But local business defeated the idea of banishing all cars from the central business district and encircling it with a motor road lined with parking garages. Most American merchants still believe that carriages, rather than traders, account for the carriage trade.

Lively, car-free shopping malls mushroomed in the suburbs, but it was not until 1964 that the first pedestrian shopping district was opened in the heart of an American city—Fresno, California. It was designed by Victor Gruen, with elaborate landscaping, or rather street-scaping, by Eckbo, Dean, Austin & Williams. It became an instant commercial and critical success. "As I write this," wrote Bernard Taper in the October 1966 *Reader's Digest*, "I am sitting contentedly, a cool drink at my elbow, right in the middle of Fulton Street—the main street of downtown Fresno, but nobody gives me a second glance. Two and a half years ago I would have been run over, arrested, or firmly led away to have my head examined. What I am doing now is simply part of the new pattern of life this bustling city has adopted: one starting from the premise that downtown is for people . . . Where there once were traffic jams, fumes, and the standard ugliness of an American city's downtown, there are now gardens, fountains, pools and numerous pieces of handsome sculpture. For the children, there are imaginative playgrounds. And for the elderly or leisurely, benches shaded by grape arbors are placed near fountains and pools."

In its first ten years, the Fresno mall generated $19.3 million in new downtown construction—23 times the city's original investment. When Knoxville, Tennessee, built its mall shortly after Fresno, a quarter of all downtown stores and offices were vacant. After the mall was completed, every square inch was gainfully occupied. The average, reasonably well-planned downtown mall, according to a recent study, more than doubles the number of visitors and sales. The pedestrian mall in Kalamazoo, Michigan, one of the earliest in this country, has increased surrounding business a steady 20 percent every year. This increased the city's overall business by 10 percent, giving momentum to a new center that includes a hotel and convention hall, to new in-town houses, vastly improved bus service, and a wildlife preservation area 15 minutes by bus from the mall.

But these success stories have still not convinced the majority of America's merchants and city fathers. At latest count, early in 1978, there were still only 70 downtown pedestrian precincts in America.

Some cities, notably Minneapolis, have compromised. A serpentine roadway reserved for slow-moving buses and taxis wiggles through Nicollet Mall in Minneapolis. It is a boon for shoppers with packages, and it does not interfere with the sense of freedom and quiet that make pedestrian malls so enjoyable. As Lawrence Halprin and his crew designed it, the winding roadway, lined with trees, benches, kiosks, and other well-designed "street furnishings," is a welcome relief from the relentlessly straight and flat midwestern street grid.

The most enchanting car-free heart of any city I know— excepting Venice, of course, which is all car-free—is the medieval heart of Munich. It was bombed to hell in Hitler's war. With postwar reconstruction came the *Wirtschafts-wunder*, automobile traffic congestion, street widenings, parking lots, high-rise buildings, downtown freeway loops, and all the other byproducts of affluence and "progress." But the *Munchner* were not happy. It did not seem worth the bother to restore the beautiful old buildings meticulously, only to drown them in pollution and ugliness. So one day late in the sixties, citizen protest stopped the latest downtown *Autobahn,* proclaimed the coming 1972 Olympics as their excuse and opportunity, built a subway and a huge downtown underground parking garage, and stopped the cars at the old city gates—the Karlstor and the Rathaustor.

Now tourists and residents in large numbers come at all hours and all seasons to shop, stroll, and linger in picturesque lanes, winding streets, and a dramatic procession of plazas amid a medley of old, new, and reconstructed buildings, some dating to the thirteenth century. The pedestrian precinct, where vehicles are allowed only for early morning deliveries and emergencies, includes the venerable Frauenkirche with its Byzantine, onion-topped spires; the imposing City Hall, a magnificent work of audacious Gothic fakery, complete with animated carillon that draws crowds every waking hour; a theater; a department store; movie houses; enough restaurants, cafes, and Bierstuben for a never-ending Oktoberfest; and two subway stations. The subway is linked to a regional rapid rail system and to the federal railroads. No point within the pedestrian precinct is more than a two or three minute walk from a bus or trolley stop, or a reasonable hope of catching a taxi.

The design of the streetscape is the result of a competition in which architects and city planners, as well as painters and sculptors, were invited to participate. In contrast to the furnishings of American pedestrian malls, which are usually cast in concrete, Munich's are light, lithe, cheery, and colorful, designed to be flexible and unobtrusive. The emphasis is not on structures that might compete visually with the buildings, but on flowers. They are grown in plastic boxes that fit the permanent planters, so fresh blooms can be exchanged for fading ones. The mall is always blossoming. There are also lots of flags and bunting, little vitrines where elegant stores display their most interesting wares, a great many pigeons, individual chairs rather than fixed benches, chairs you move into the sun or the shade, together for conversation or apart for solitude. Several fountains splash and gush and sprinkle.

The best thing I found in this human heart of Munich was the sound of people laughing, the din of people talking, and pigeons gurgling and flapping their wings, and the sound of playing fountains.

That brings me to noise in the city—the visual as well as the audible noise, the constant assault on our eyes and ears. Munich's car-free center is pleasantly stimulating and I found this true even in icy fog and drizzle. But for all the stimulation and variety, you are always oriented. In American downtown centers you are invariably confused and irritated. Munich has but one directional sign for every ten on a New York or Washington or Cincinnatti downtown street.

On a single downtown block in America I have counted as many as 23 directional, safety and information signs, to say nothing of traffic lights, poles, posts, standards, parking meters, police call boxes, fire alarm boxes, mail deposit boxes, fire hydrants, bus stop signs, trash cans, and trash. The jumble overwhelms and bewilders you. The redundancy numbs you. You don't, you can't pay any attention.

Whereupon the city puts up more signs—bigger, flashier, and flashing signs and signals—to numb or to irritate even more. It is the same with noise.

There have been a few attempts in this country to clean up the jungle of street graphics and give us clear, articulate signs and signals to tell us where we are, where to find where we want to go, and what to do or not to do for our safety and that of everyone else, such as we find in Munich and most other European cities.

But these attempts—in New Haven or on Washington's Tenth Street Mall—have been mostly inept. American graphic designers, like so many American architects, like to be original and fashionable rather than good and efficient. They go in for the latest fashion rather than the simplest and most appropriate design. The latest fashion in lettering, as I write, is to squeeze letters together so that you have a blur rather than a word, and to use a typeface called "Helvetica," which has even thickness, simple form, and little legibility. As a result, these demonstration projects demonstrated nothing in particular and led nowhere.

We have done better with graphic information at airports and some large shopping centers, and lately at the Washington National Zoo and other branches of the Smithsonian Institution. This just happened because people with taste and visual sensibility were in charge. The people in charge of our street and highway signs and street furnishings are mostly engineers who had no training in graphics and don't care. They still resist the international pictogram system, although it is finally making some inroads on American highways. But there is as yet not much of a public demand for getting rid of the sign clutter and making our cities and highways intelligible.

The same is true of noise pollution. It has gotten so bad that most people do not even hear it any more. City noise, according to the U.S. Environmental Protection Agency, "is a growing menace, not just to boilermakers and jackhammer operators, but to all of us." The danger is scientifically established. Excessive noise causes the pupils to dilate, small blood vessels to constrict, digestion to slow, breathing to quicken, the pulse to race, the blood pressure to rise, glucose to pour into the blood stream, secretion of adrenalin to increase, and muscles to tense.

The result of these anatomical events can be headaches, insomnia, ulcers, kidney trouble, sexual impotence, heart and circulatory disease, and, in the opinion of some responsible physicians, adverse effects on unborn children. Humans react in two ways to noise: they either explode, become aggressive, distrustful, and irritable, or they implode, wreaking havoc within themselves. The first reaction may land them in jail, the second in a mental hospital. Admissions to mental hospitals from high-noise areas, especially near airports, is 29 to 31 percent higher than in low-noise neighborhoods.

Cities have always been noisy. The noise of night traffic was so bad in ancient Rome that, as one historian put it, "it would snatch sleep from a seacalf and even the Emperor Claudius himself." But it is worse—and unhealthier—today, because not only do we have noisy machines, such as vacuum cleaners indoors and trucks outdoors, but we have also introduced noise to fight noise. "Beat it with Muzak," seems to be our slogan, as we douse ourselves in incessant sound, dulling our senses as with drugs.

The drugging goes on just about everywhere we go. Muzak—by which I mean not just the specific brand of taped concoctions of musical mush without beginning or end, but all manner of incessant electronic music from tape recorders or radios—douses you at airports, train stations, in stores, restaurants, taxis, and even outdoors in shopping malls and streets. This inures people not to respond to noise any more. I have heard burglar alarms ring and ring and ring for hours on end in my alley or down the street. Nobody paid the slightest attention, including, I fear, the burglar.

City noises must be controlled and reduced as urgently as the air must be cleaned. The main obstacle is people. Truck drivers believe noisy trucks have more power. Housewives, according to industry surveys, have the same mistaken faith in the motors of noisy vacuum cleaners. Nevertheless, the health of a noise sensitive minority (or is it a silent majority?) must be protected. Chicago's Noise Control Ordinance, which gives the manufacturers of trucks and other noisy machines sufficient time to develop quieter models, is setting an example for the nation.

But ordinances must be enforced. And enforcement can only be forced by public demand. Public demand is created by increased public awareness. We need at least as much noise about noise as we are making about nicotine. Noise is hazardous to your health.

If the city were quieter, we would not have to take charter flights to Munich to hear the fountains play.

25 For Lovers and for Friends

To hear the fountains, we must first clear some streets and plazas of cars. Now that we appear to have gotten over the notion that the only way to the American dream is a ten-lane freeway, this is no longer as difficult as it seemed.

Let me state the obvious first: The automobile is a marvelous invention that has given a large portion of humanity a new freedom to move about at will and see and enjoy the world. I usually rent a car when I travel to do just that—to have freedom.

But conversely, as we agreed in the last chapter, we don't want to be slaves to that marvelous invention. We need to get organized about transportation, see what means of transportation are at our disposal and what each of these means can do best, and see how to make it easy for each mode of transportation to move at its greatest efficiency.

We are not that rational in this country. We are wasteful and inefficient. It is inefficient, for instance, to use big jets to travel from New York to Washington, or from San Francisco to Los Angeles. On these trips, big jets are hardly up at their proper cruising height before they have to get down again. It would be far more efficient to make intercity trips by fast train—direct from downtown to downtown—and use jets for trans- or intercontinental flights.

For various complicated reasons, however, we let our

railroads and roadbeds go to hell. The so-called fast train on the New York-Washington run isn't very fast, shakes so badly you can't read, let alone work, and is rudely unreliable. People therefore take the shuttle and clutter up air and airports with far too many noisy and polluting airplanes.

The most efficient mode of commuting and otherwise getting around within an urban region is rapid rail transit. It is efficient, that is, if it is backed by a good feeder system of buses, mini-buses, or shared rides of any other kind, which take commuters from their scattered suburban homes to the rapid transit station. There must also be adequate free parking at the suburban station.

A regional rapid rail system, like Metrorail in Washington or BART, the Bay Area Rapid Transit system, in San Francisco, is expensive. Part of its efficiency is that it runs underground in the city, and tunneling costs a lot of money. But it is costly compared to what? The only alternatives are more freeways for more cars and buses. In urban areas freeways alone, however, as highway advocates usually forget to mention, are as expensive as subways. The proposed Westway along the Hudson in New York City will cost $250 million a mile. Add to that the actual and social cost of displacing people, places of employment, and buildings; the cost (and displacement) for still more parking in the city; the costs of jamming still more cars on city streets; the costs of commuting time; the lives and limbs lost in highway accidents; and the costs of pollution. And all that still doesn't say anything about the comparative cost of energy consumption. It may seem negligible today. But what about 25 years from now?

The trouble with the rail transit discussions in Washington, Baltimore, Atlanta, San Francisco, Los Angeles, and other cities where subways are being built or planned, is that they are only seemingly informed. The urban highway systems, built during the 1950s and '60s, showed little concern for cost or economic impact because a generous federal government paid 90 percent out of an unlimited highway trust fund constantly refilled with gasoline tax. On the other hand, urban rail transit must be approved by local voters and is therefore carefully (and rightly) scrutinized by economists and traffic engineers. The scrutinizers, however, as Louis J. Gambaccini, manager of the New York Port Authority Trans-Hudson Corporation has pointed out, "are obsessively capable of identifying the costs, but singularly unsuccessful in quantifying the broad range of benefits that transit contributes to the society it serves."

We need buses. A great deal can and must be done to improve their efficiency, comfort, and the reliability of their service. Cities that have seriously tried to regain lost public confidence in the bus system—by providing bus shelters, separate lanes for buses, more attractive vehicles, more polite drivers, fare reductions, more routes, and more reliable service—have, in some instances, had spectacular increases in the number of riders.

The problem with buses is twofold. One: no bus is faster than the car ahead of it. In other words, the bus is subject to the same traffic jam as the commuter car. The only answer here is separate lanes, or, better still, routes. Just marking the bus lane does not help, because cars will sneak in anyway. Wouldn't you? Building lane separations works only on multilane freeways. It can't be done on city streets. Some cities have created separate routes for buses during rush hour by closing certain streets to cars. The people in those cars cuss, of course, but it works well for the people in the buses.

The second problem is that a lot of buses and drivers are needed during rush hour, but a good number of these drivers must then be paid for idling during off-hours. The only way to overcome this cost inefficiency is for the transit authority to hire part-time drivers. But drivers' unions are loath to agree to that.

Bus drivers' unions do agree, however, to fare-free rides. This attracts more customers, and the necessary government subsidies assure good, steady wages. The first city to offer free bus rides downtown was Seattle. The service started in 1973, and is available 24 hours a day, seven days a week. The passenger can board any bus in the free downtown zone and if he gets off before the bus leaves the zone, there is no charge. Beyond the zone, regular fares apply. The result has been a 200 percent increase in daily bus trips into the downtown area and a corresponding decrease of the number of cars downtown. There has also been a marked increase in downtown business. The annual operating cost of the free service is surprisingly small—$138,132 in 1978, according to the Department of Transportation. Denver and Trenton also give free bus rides. It is entirely possible that the country will soon come to consider urban transportation an essential utility that should be paid for out of general taxes—like roads for trucks and automobiles— rather than individual fares that do not cover the entire cost, anyway.

We are also learning that regional rapid rail and buses are not enough. We need what transportation planner jargon calls Automated Guideway Transit, or AGT, as well as Paratransit. In English this means holding on to our old trolleys, in one form or another. It also includes taxis, (with more efficient cabs).

We need trolleys because buses leapfrog and bunch up. You wait and wait and wait, particularly when it rains or snows. Finally, three or four buses, playing choo-choo train, come all at once. The only way to avoid this are the above-mentioned separate bus lanes or routes, which are not always practical. A streetcar or trolley has its own, built-in lane, known as a rail. It runs on electricity and is therefore more energy-efficient and less polluting than the combustion engine bus. It can also run faster and carry more passengers. All this makes its comeback quite likely, particularly for commuting. Traffic engineers, pretending they never heard of a trolley, call for Light Rail Vehicles, or LRVs. Never mind, they will clang just as sweet.

In fact, in Detroit of all places, restored 1890 trolleys are already clanging. The federal Urban Mass Transportation Administration and the state of Michigan got together and bought six lovely, fire-engine-red trolley cars in Portugal. Their job is to attract tourists to Washington Boulevard and take them to Cobo Hall convention center.

Other varieties of AGTs, for reasons known only to

transportation planners, are also called "people movers." Some are fantasies and others can be seen in amusement parks, world's fairs, airports, and Sunday supplements.

An example of the fantasy people movers are little golf carts that can be driven from home to the freeway, where they are linked to hundreds of other little golf carts to form a train that shoots downtown like the Japanese Tokaido line. Downtown the golf carts disassemble again and are driven straight to one's office.

Other people movers stay on their tracks, which are elevated above the street so they won't interfere with the traffic below. Only the supporting columns do. Which is why New York City removed its people mover, known as the Third Avenue El, more than thirty years ago, and sold it to the Japanese. The Japanese melted it and shot it back in World War II in the form of bombs and bullets.

At this writing only a very few people movers have escaped from amusement parks, world's fairs, airports, or Sunday supplements. One went to Morgantown, West Virginia, and was never heard from again. Another is about to establish itself in Houston. It will run on a 1.098-mile north-south route on Milam Street, at an estimated cost of $40 million. If it gets an estimated 24,000 Houstonian commuters out of their cars to ride the thing it should "recapture $10 million from the value generated." The Houston people mover will be different from the Third Avenue El that ran in the middle of the street. The Houston El runs along the side and blightens only the sidewalk.

Taxi service—pardon, Paratransit—is not only a convenience for well-to-do people in a hurry. It is essential to those who cannot use other means of public transportation (because there isn't any, or because they are too old, too young, or disabled), and those who don't drive or can't afford to own cars. That adds up to a great many people.

It is therefore unfortunate that the taxi cab industry is in bad shape. Since 1974, about 1,000 cab companies a year have gone out of business across the country. The reason is that insurance costs, gasoline prices, and other expenses have gone up and up, and fares could not be increased fast enough to make up for these increases. What is more, taxi vehicles in this country are uncomfortable and inefficient. Except for the Checker cab, which is expensive and, according to some drivers, no longer what it used to be, there aren't any specially designed taxicabs. The automobile manufacturers don't care because they don't see a market.

The federal government, for all these reasons, is trying to help put taxis back on the road. The Department of Transportation is, first of all, trying to impress local governments with the fact that taxis, jitney service, dial-a-ride, community minibuses, and other forms of shared and flexible transportation, are as important as bus and rail transit on fixed routes. Taxis account for 40 percent of all public transportation. They are especially needed in thinly settled suburbs and rural areas and must be included in sensible, overall transportation plans.

Taxis can go far to supplement bus service. The Miami Transit Authority, for instance, has discontinued bus service at night. Instead, on call, it sends a taxi that charges the regular bus fare and reimburses the cab company for the rest. The customer gets home. The transit authority keeps its riders. The cabs have a steady contract. And the whole arrangement costs half of what night time bus service would cost.

Some social agencies maintain their own fleet of cars to take their "clients" around. Usually this is more expensive, however, than contracting a taxi company. The Red Cross does this in various cities to everyone's satisfaction. Other social service agencies provide taxi coupons for the elderly, handicapped, and others under their care. The government subsidizes such services if there is a real need. Some states pay gasoline tax rebates. The federal government should do the same. Cities should ease needless restrictions on cabs and encourage rather than prohibit jitney services. If that competes with buses and trolleys, all the better. We need competition to keep service up and fares down.

The federal transportation agency has also developed a prototype for an ideal paratransit vehicle. It is a small car that comfortably accommodates four persons, one of them in a wheelchair. A fold-up ramp allows the person in the wheelchair to board without assistance. The vehicle is supposed to be quiet and nonpolluting, and the hope is that something like it will be mass-produced before long. With 13 million handicapped and even more elderly people and youngsters unable to drive, there can be no question about a huge market.

Another mode of transportation that needs more help and recognition by government is the bicycle. In America, it has grown in less than a decade from a child's toy to a popular, adult way of travel. An estimated 100 million Americans own bicycles, and more bicycles than cars have been produced in the past few years. What these bicyclists need are more bicycle paths or at least sidewalk lanes. They also need more secure bicycle parking. Chaining bicycles to a sign post provides little protection. Thieves have a variety of tools that can cut a lock or chain in 30 seconds. There are, however, theft and vandal proof parking devices, and it should be made mandatory for public buildings, apartment houses, shopping centers, large factories and offices to provide them. In some communities, bikes can now be carried on buses and minibuses.

Much must be done to keep all of this moving more smoothly. An easy way to gain two more traffic lanes on downtown streets is to ban parking, no matter how loud the merchants scream. Downtown parking rates should be increased wherever public transportation is available.

Another device to keep traffic moving is gliding traffic lights,

or "signal progression," as the engineers call it. This keeps cars
moving at a given speed with a minimum of red lights. In Berlin
and a few other cities, nine out of ten street intersections are
blocked off at least during rush hour, turning avenues into
limited access highways. Motorists who need to cross or enter
these highways need only to drive up or down a few side streets.
Reversible one-way streets also help a great deal—one way
toward downtown in the morning, one way suburb-bound in
the evening.

In Washington, different government departments have
different work schedules to ease rush hour congestion. In
several West German cities, large corporations give their
employees a choice of working hours. The Germans call this
gleitende Arbeitszeit, and the system not only eases rush hour
traffic, but the lives of the employees as well. Early risers can
start early and get to their gardens or the tennis court sooner.
Parents can take their children to school before they report to
work. Though everyone works a regular eight-hour shift, the
factory or office runs for 12 hours a day.

Car-free public spaces need not be the elaborate affairs they
usually are. In residential districts it helps to close a street to
automobiles with a few bollards or planters and use it as a
playground, market, or park. It can even be done for just part of
the day. In Bedford-Stuyvesant, architect I. M. Pei designed a
miniplaza, complete with fountain, benches, sandboxes, and
trees, on half a residential street, and turned the other half into a
parking lot for the residents. Cars are parked perpendicularly,
rather than parallel to the curb. In Delft, Holland, such park-
and-play streets are called "townyards."

In short, it is time that we stop assuming that it is the God-
given right of every combustion engine to move and stand
anywhere it pleases. We should, as mentioned earlier, shift the
emphasis from transportation planning to antitransportation
planning. We should apply the principles of new town planning
to existing suburbs and arrange things so that people can stay
put and spend a minimum of time and energy on travel.

This means, to start with, that planners plan for communities

rather than just housing. In the communities, or neighborhoods, every home or apartment should be in walking distance
of an elementary school, a small supermarket, a branch library,
and a neighborhood center.

The neighborhoods would be clustered around a district
center, a satellite downtown, which includes a high school, a
larger shopping center, a department store, a movie theater,
and the like. Several districts, in turn, are grouped around
downtown, with its specialty shops, operas, theaters, museums,
big department stores, hospitals, universities, central library,
big office buildings, city vibrations, and celebrations.

The logical transport links are from home to neighborhood
center on foot or bicycle, from neighborhood center to district
center by rapid rail. This leaves the automobile for pleasure—a
luxury rather than a necessity.

This urban hierarchy is an oversimplified scheme to suggest a
desirable order. Life is not that orderly, thank heaven. The
living city is built on topography, on tradition, on whim, and on
accident. Good planning is not schematic, but organic, which,
in Mumford's words, "must not only seek a structural answer to
every function of the city, but it must also express, as fully as
possible, both in the surface plan and the design of the
buildings, the needs and the ideal purposes of the community,
conserving past forms that are still serviceable while preparing
to accomodate future needs."

One imperative future need is to reduce and eventually to
eliminate the destructive, antiurban impact of automobile
dependency. We admire Venice, not only for its beauty—
marred, but not really diminished by pollution and decay—but
for the very reason that people can enjoy this beauty
undisturbed by noisy vehicles. Venice is the only large city in the
world where humans and combustion engines do not interfere
with one another. Transport of people and goods is confined to
gondolas, barges, and other boats, moving on canals undisturbed by foot traffic. The canals are subject to a logical
hierarchy of use and speed. Motorboats and water buses, the
vaporetti, move relatively fast on the Grand Canal. Gondolas

and small barges distribute the traffic more finely on noisy middle-sized and quiet narrow canals into the various precincts. No one is far from transportation. Yet, Venetian life is lived on tranquil islands.

The same principle can be applied to cities on land if we heed the advice Lewis Mumford gave a convention of the American Institute of Architects some years ago. "If you are thinking of the culture of cities," Mumford said, "forget about the damn motor car and plan cities on the human scale for lovers and for friends."

26 Large Is Inevitable

To plan cities on the human scale, their social and economic problems must be attacked on the regional scale. City problems can no longer be solved within city boundaries. While the cities have most of the unemployed, the states have most of the power, and the federal government has most of the money. The need for regional planning and action in no way contradicts the need to strengthen the sense and institution of neighborhood, both in the city and in the suburbs. Being herd animals, we like to live in small settlements rather than in isolation. We like to bring our children up in villages—rural, urban, or suburban. And we enjoy—and probably need—the interdependence, companionship, and sense of belonging that neighborhood offers. Living directly in the big city, without contact between people who live on the same apartment house floor, can be as lonely as living on a mountain top.

But neighborhoods are not islands. City and regional traffic flows through them, city and regional services sustain them. And, conversely, only the city and the region can supply the education, employment, cultural institutions, recreation, and specialties that one small neighborhood could not possibly support.

In short, there cannot be a happy neighborhood life as long as urban life as a whole remains ecologically irresponsible, economically wasteful, and socially unjust.

So, while small is beautiful, "large is inevitable," as Wilfred Owen says. Owen has pondered these things in the scholarly calm of The Brookings Institution. We must think, plan, make policy, legislate, fund, and build, in Owen's words, "not for the old city, not for the legal city, but the city that is the real city—the emerging regional city."

Almost 80 percent of our population lives in this real city, the emerging regional city, with its racial and economic separation of people. And they will continue to live there for the foreseeable future.

It is what the Census Bureau calls a "metropolitan area." The term was invented many years ago and denotes one or more large cities which, together with their surrounding suburbs, have formed an urban agglomeration—the British call it "conurbation"—with a total population of 200,000 or more.

The political boundaries, separation, and segregation within the metropolitan areas have become serious obstacles to the welfare not only of the people in the inner city, but also of those living in the suburbs. Worse than economic malfunction and the health hazards due to pollution is that "our nation is moving toward two societies, one black, one white—separate and unequal," as the Kerner Commission, which investigated the civil disorders during the summer of 1967, so bluntly stated.

This fact, I fear, has not changed since the 1967 riots. It is only tempered a little because a small segment of the black population has since moved up and out of the ghetto.

What has changed is that the suburbs are, for the most part, no longer the suburbs they were ten years ago. They are no longer just dormitories for people who commute to the center

city. They are developing employment, shopping centers, and medical services. Less than half the "suburban" population now works in the center city. The majority makes a living elsewhere in the metropolitan area. Since the end of World War II, roughly three-quarters of the country's economic and population growth has taken place in these newly urbanized territories that we still call suburbs and that are in reality a vastly expanded city—the megacity. True suburbs, the idyllic kind on the end of streetcar lines, are almost extinct.

Automobiles obliterated urban boundaries. Air and water pollution never respected them. Nor does water supply, the job market, or, for that matter, anything except exclusionary zoning. What Owen calls "the real city" is a huge organism in which, as in all organisms, every part is dependent on all other parts. But that does not work so well if the interdependent parts are separate and unequal.

You can't have efficient fire protection unless the various fire departments in the metropolitan area work together. You can't fight crime effectively if the police force is divided into dozens of separate commands, taking their orders from different chiefs who, more often than not, do not care to cooperate.

The District of Columbia government used to let people die of heart attacks on its streets, rather than allow nearby Virginia ambulances especially equipped for cardiac emergencies to cross the city boundary. This particularly cruel idiocy has been remedied. Many other, equally absurd consequences of urban America's balkanization have not.

One of them, discussed earlier in the context of city living, is our severe circulatory problems. They are due to an unbalanced and uncoordinated transportation system. Our freeways and beltways move automobiles quite well—too well, in fact. In the absence, or near-absence, of other transportation, however, these arteries pour an excess of cars and trucks into the city, clogging it to the point of cardiospasm. What is more, they are of no use to the inner-city poor, who can find work only out in the region, but don't have the cars to get there. The circulatory system, in short, does not work properly. It does not really pulsate the region's lifeblood throughout the region's body. And for all its federally financed arteries, it lacks the local capillaries—minibuses and other devices, or even pleasant walkways—to keep the region's parks, scenic areas, playfields, and small shopping and employment centers readily accessible and lively.

The lack, or extreme difficulty of access to so many things life could so easily offer, increases dependency on what is almost universally available in America—television.

There is surely a direct relationship between this opiate of the people and the sad decline of education in this country. What is more, if suburban youngsters could get more easily and freely to museums, public libraries, sports, the outdoors, amusement parks, and the bustle of people who don't live in their own kind of suburban subdivision, they would be, without doubt, intellectually more stimulated and more interested in speaking, reading, and writing.

It is amazing what my generation of city children could see and learn just by walking to school. The view from a suburban school bus window is pretty dull by comparison.

Nor do ghetto schools offer much hope of educating their students out of the ghetto. A school can only teach as much as the majority of its students is capable of learning.

The key to most of this is a more equitable and rational distribution of people within the regional city. This means mainly giving people who now live in the inner city the opportunity to move to what once were called suburbs, where they can more easily find jobs and send their children to better schools.

The balkanization of the regional city makes this virtually impossible, however. Each little jurisdiction in the regional city—and the New York metropolitan area has over 1,300— now has the de facto power of zoning (de jure the power belongs to the states, but they delegated it). Each little jurisdiction therefore zones in its own narrow interest. In the suburbs, that interest is to keep things as they are and, at all costs, keep poor people out.

This is not always bigoted racism. It is also dismal ignorance and disinterest in the larger issues involved in planning. There is no way, as matters stand, for the average citizen to get involved. "The family in a central city apartment that would like to 'graduate' to a modest suburban house is not party to suburban zoning hearings, nor aware that sewer moratoriums affect its interest," wrote Herbert M. Franklin, a well-known lawyer and housing consultant. "The suburban homeowner does not recognize that the location of a new industrial plant in a neighboring suburb, or that suburb's exclusionary housing policy, may create a surge of modest-income housing construction in *his* area, over-loading *his* schools. The system is therefore invisible to those who are most disadvantaged by it and thus retards the emergence of the political consensus to do anything about it.

"Accordingly, urban land has rarely been the focus of political grievance in American society. It has . . . seldom been regarded as a resource that could itself be used to improve other facets of urban life."

The federal government has tried repeatedly to locate subsidized housing outside the center city. It has, in some instances, made housing subsidies and other federal grants dependent on a "fair share" distribution of subsidized housing throughout the metropolitan area. Some suburban counties have been reasonable about it, mainly because the cost of housing has increased to such an extent that only half of all American families can afford to buy a house of their own. Housing subsidies are needed not only for poor black families, but also to keep school teachers near their schools, firemen near their firehouses, and sales clerks near the shopping centers.

The courts have failed to support the fair distribution of subsidized housing. In almost all instances where the attempt was challenged, the courts have upheld the right of local zoning boards to deny construction of apartment houses, increased densities, or whatever other subterfuge could be found to exclude "undesirable" newcomers.

In June 1976, in the so-called "Eastlake Decision," the

Supreme Court under Chief Justice Warren E. Burger held that even if 55 percent of the voters approved, a zoning board can refuse low-cost housing. It was a terrifying victory for continued urban disorder.

But urban order is hard to achieve in America, because political jurisdictions seldom coincide with economic and urban realities. Our settlements all but completely disregard city, county, and state boundaries.

What is more, the only people who can restructure our urbanized regions are the city and county council members and the state legislators who have a vested interest in the existing arrangement. We have had regional planning commissions for years—and the politicians have ignored them for years.

Special regional authorities have been established to take care of special regional needs, such as the Port of New York Authority, the Washington (D.C.) Metropolitan Area Transit Authority, airport authorities, or water authorities. In most instances, they do their jobs well enough. They often collect their own taxes and have the tendency to push their special concerns ahead of other concerns. The Port of New York Authority, for instance, has for years consistently favored private automobiles (which pay it bridge and tunnel tolls) over improvements and extensions of public transportation. The authority finally relented and allowed a subway to be built to La Guardia and Kennedy airports.

More promising are councils of governments, associations of representatives of all the political jurisdictions within a metropolitan region. At least they talk about the entire region's problems. But seldom can they get their people on the city and county councils back home to agree on more than the easy, technical things, like regional police teleprinters or pooling ambulance service. Most of them don't even talk about the tough ones—rational distribution of factories and other employment centers, the use of land, and who may live next to whom.

On this continent, we have actual regional government only in Toronto, Canada. The weak regional governments of Miami

(Dade County), Jacksonville, and Nashville function only nominally.

What works well, however, is the Metropolitan Council of the Twin Cities Area. It lords over the cities of Minneapolis and St. Paul, seven suburban counties, and 300 smaller units of local government. It was created by an enlightened Minnesota state legislature in 1967, appointed by the governor, financed by a special levy on local tax income, and given jurisdiction over regional sewage and waste disposal, pollution control, comprehensive transportation planning, airport development control, and regional parks and open spaces.

The Minnesota legislature has given Twin Cities regional planners the power to enforce what they plan. They can locate schools, sewers, shopping centers, and the like. Business will know what to expect and can make investments accordingly. The point is to concentrate development within the metropolitan area and thereby save an estimated $2 billion in the next dozen years on roads, sewers, and other expenses of urban sprawl.

Minneapolis-St. Paul has no really tough problems, except for a few unhappy Indians. Minnesota is a homogeneous state. The example of Minneapolis does not apply in multistate urban regions, such as New York (which includes parts of the states of New York, New Jersey, and Connecticut), or Washington (which includes the District of Columbia, Maryland, and Virginia). Even most states, for that matter, would let us down.

"The ability to break through locally sanctioned economic and racial segregation is so important," wrote Herbert Franklin, "that reliance on state action as the only triggering mechanism would be illusory."

Franklin therefore proposes that Congress charter a national metropolitan development corporation as a quasi-independent public authority. The corporation would provide funds for local metropolitan development corporations to purchase land in advance for orderly future growth—land needed for housing, public works, open space, parks, outdoor recreation, and other urban essentials. It would establish standards for a good living environment within its metropolitan region. It would act as the conduit for all federal funds now distributed to metropolitan areas by the Departments of Housing and Urban Development; Transportation; Health, Education and Welfare; the Environmental Protection Agency; and the other 17 federal agencies which, as of early 1978, administered 187 programs concerned with community development.

Franklin's federal corporation would also conduct research, monitor performance, keep policies and standards flexible and up-to-date, and move in as "developer of last resort" in metropolitan areas that do not have their own development corporation.

The local metropolitan development corporation would be similar to the British new town corporations and the quasi-government New York State Urban Development Corporation. It must be endowed with the power of government, including the power of eminent domain and the authority to override exclusionist and archaic local zoning and building codes. It would be not only a planning, but also a *building* agency.

The corporation's foremost objective is to work toward the orderly development and redevelopment of the regional city. This may call for building integrated new satellite towns as well as smaller, integrated communities, or what planners call Planned Unit Development, or PUD. As we have seen earlier, only a developer endowed with governmental powers can assemble and purchase the land in the proper location, including sufficient land for open space, recreation and greenbelts. Only the governmental power can fit the new communities efficiently into the network of roads and rails, sewer lines and water mains, and assure that the communities are from the start, served by elementary schools, day-care centers, community centers, basic shopping, and recreation.

The regional development corporation would be required to synchronize all its activities. As it redevelops or rehabilitates a center city neighborhood to attract middle-income office workers back into the city, it must simultaneously build new homes for the displaced low-income people. This displacement housing should be built in the suburbs and in integrated communities with good schools and good opportunities for job training and jobs.

The corporation would also be charged with the advance acquisition of sites for such key regional institutions as high schools and colleges, sewer treatment plants, hospitals, airports, research centers, and regional parks and peoples' parks. The latter would follow the example of socialist countries where virtually very big city has a combination recreation and cultural park.

(The most enchanting downtown cultural park in the West is Copenhagen's Tivoli. On this continent, I most enjoyed Ontario Place in Toronto, Canada. It combines natural beauty and the art of horticulture with all sorts of interesting exhibits, concerts, theaters, movies, amusements, imaginative playgrounds for people of all ages, rowing and swimming, dancing, public ceremonies, and a variety of restaurants and eateries for different tastes and pocketbooks.)

Most everyone nowadays, I am sure, is skeptical about governmental enterprises. As Franklin points out, "most of us have confronted governmental bureaucracies that either run wild, seemingly untamed by any responsiveness to the people, or that languish in a torpor suggesting they are thinly disguised welfare programs for increasingly uncivil nonservants."

Yet we certainly cannot expect free enterprise to undo the urban chaos that all too free enterprise created. Nor can the task be performed by powerless, bankrupt cities, unwilling states, or the willing, but frustrated debating societies of councils of governments. This leaves only the federal government, but since the task cuts across the jurisdictions of virtually all existing agencies, a new one for just this purpose is essential. As Franklin points out, we came close to doing what is here proposed with Franklin D. Roosevelt's New Deal National Resources Planning Board and Public Works Administration of the 1930s.

Far from competing with, or preempting private enterprise

and initiative, regional development corporations would encourage them. New York's UDC works most constructively with private architects, consultants, and builders. It has shown ingenuity, an air of freshness and idealism not seen in this country since the early New Deal.

To quote Franklin once more: "New institutions could respond to the needs of the majority of American households who are priced out of a better living environment in the metropolitan heartland. They could open up individual choice that the system now restricts. They could enable private enterprise to meet more effectively than it can now, the social and environmental goals for a metropolitan society."

27 Neighborhood

The fabled old homestead consisted of three generations of a family living together. It took care of most essential functions of life. As our undoubtedly romanticized legends have it, everyone had his or her job and place: The parents worked in the fields. Grandmother took care of the very young, knitted, and sewed, while grandfather whittled. Children herded the geese or goats. The old folks told stories, and the young folks sang songs. There was a family altar or an icon in the living room.

Food, education, cultural continuity, religion—all came together around the hearth. They came together to make life whole—indeed, to make life possible. On their own, humans are the most helpless of creatures. (Romulus and Remus and Kaspar Hauser had to be nursed by wolves.)

As settlements became larger, human life supports spread out from the homestead into the community. But they remained within walking distance. It obviously would not do to live too far from the water well, the baker, the school, the chapel, fields to play in, and woods to neck in.

In antiquity, the Middle Ages, the Renaissance, and the early industrial age, daily urban life was still lived in walkable communities or neighborhoods. They were the nuclei of any city. In the early industrial city, working-class neighborhoods, helped by ward heelers and their political machines, assimilated immigrants and rural in-migrants. Neighborhoods became instruments of civilization, although when the blacks came, racism blunted the instrument.

With the automobile, mobility, electronic communication, the segregation of urban functions, and urban sprawl, neighborhood dissipated in the vast anonymity of the regional city. Only the very poor, unable to own cars and telephones and to move out with the rest, were able to hold on to neighborhood.

While the Modern movement, idolizing all technological development, hastened the disintegration of neighborhood, the Ebenezer Howard-Lewis Mumford school of urban thought tried to preserve and strengthen it as the basic unit in the urban order, the cell in the urban organism.

The most widely accepted definition of a neighborhood is that which city planner Clarence Arthur Perry set forth in 1929, in his contribution to the "Regional Plan for New York and Its Environs." The neighborhood, Perry wrote, is a residential district of sufficient size to support an elementary school. That would be a population of from 3,000 to 10,000 people.

Perry's concept was adapted by Sir Patrick Abercrombie in his London Plan of 1943, which, in turn, influenced the planning of new towns in England and around the world. As new towns evolved, there was experimentation with the size, the services, and the demographic makeup of neighborhoods. There is no ideal formula. There is no agreement on what constitutes an ideal neighborhood. Nor should there be. What is the ideal height of a tree, the ideal smell of a flower?

Neighborhoods evolve out of topography, history, economics, the way people wish to live. They are constantly changing. There is just one common denominator: For a neighborhood to be a neighborhood and to form neighborhood ties, the basic necessities of life ought to be within easy walking distance. It is awfully difficult to relate to others and feel neighborly while driving an automobile.

What are the basic necessities of life? Certainly food stores. Certainly an elementary school with a playground. There must be a neighborhood meeting place, either in the school or church, or in a recreation center that also houses community activities. If there is no lake or river, there should be a public swimming pool. There must be laundromats, dry cleaners, a tavern or two. There ought to be a park. Parks are the lungs of the city.

It is best if the neighborhood coincides with the election precinct and the police precinct. It should also contain a fire station and a post office. In short, ideally the neighborhood should be a clear, complete, and consistent political and administrative entity with some degree of self-determination and representation in city hall.

The high school, a movie, good restaurants, hardware stores, a health clinic, municipal services, might be made available on the next higher, or district level. But, again, there can be no formula or prescription. A neighborhood is what has historically become a neighborhood, or what feels like a neighborhood to those who live there. My only rule for

neighborhoods is that they are large enough to avoid intrusive familiarity, and small enough to seem personal. It is a place, to borrow Margaret Mead's phrase, in which "human beings— fragmented by bureaucracies, mass production, impersonal decision making on a scale so large that decisions have become increasingly dehumanized—can be made whole again."

If this sounds a bit mystical, it is. How do you define the mysterious sense of "feeling at home?"

The virtues of neighborhood were rediscovered by Jane Jacobs in her book I mentioned earlier, *The Death and Life of Great American Cities,* first published in 1961. Since Jacobs rediscovered *old* neighborhoods, notably Greenwich Village, she did not notice that Ebenezer Howard, Lewis Mumford, and the Garden City movement urged a way to embody the old neighborhood spirit and old neighborhood values in new, new town neighborhoods. It escaped her, because she mistakenly assumed the Garden City people were against the city, and she hated them for it.

More recently, neighborhood was rediscovered by both the "ethnics" or "hard-hats" (formerly known as "the working class)," and "young professionals" (formerly known as the "middle-class intelligentsia").

The hard-hats got angry when red-lining accelerated the deterioration of their neighborhoods and the federal bulldozers threatened to turn their homes into high-rise projects or highways. They got angry when, after the inner-city riots, they thought (without much justification) that blacks got all the breaks and that black neighborhoods were given more federal assistance than their own. They might have moved out to suburbia. But rising costs blocked the old escape. They had to stay and fight.

Sociologist Nathan Glazer and ex-sociologist Daniel Patrick Moynihan, as well as an inner-city priest named Monsignor Geno C. Baroni, also had something to do with it.

In the early 1960s, Glazer and Moynihan looked at the much praised melting pot and found that it did not melt. Jews, Italians, Irish, and other ethnic groups may have increased their incomes and therefore their status; they may even have moved out of their ghettos to where the rent is higher and the garbage gets picked up more frequently. But they do not thereby turn into Wasps. They do not care to turn into Wasps. They resist melting, reinforced by matzos, pasta, and Irish whiskey.

Americans change their myths for new credos with remarkable ease and speed. As soon as it became apparent that the melting pot had never even simmered, we cooked up a new Great American ideal—Pluralism.

It was suddenly quite red-white-and-blue to be just as ethnic as you wanted to, bursting with black pride and Polish pride, Lithuanian songs, Ukrainian folk dances, German sauerkraut, Mexican enchiladas, Greek moussaka, and other manifestations of unmelted diversity. So here was another good reason to preserve the center city neighborhoods—New York's "Little Italys" and Detroit's "Greek Towns"—as cherished reservations of ethnicity.

Monsignor Baroni emerged from the Washington slums at the right time with the skill to turn an uneasy emotion into an important political act. He made Archie Bunker tolerant, at least on the surface. "If you want to stay in the city and improve your neighborhoods," he told the angry hard-hats in effect, "you have to learn to get along with blacks and chicanos. In fact, if you want to get anywhere, you have to form a political coalition with them."

With the help of the Catholic hierarchy and foundation grants to finance conferences, workshops, and studies, he did it—not by condemning racism, but by conceding that white ethnics in the city center have legitimate complaints. The remedy, he said, was not black-white polarization, but cooperation. Tolerance, he quoted René Dubos as saying, is more than a virtue; it is a requirement for survival.

Baroni and his coalition deserve much of the credit for pressuring Congress into making red-lining a federal offense, and making neighborhood preservation a federal policy.

The American labor movement was nowhere to be seen while the monsignor fought his battles to help working-class neighborhoods help cities. But Baroni kept stressing that as more and more parishes and neighborhoods die, "we will enter a new era of American apartheid, urban ghettos surrounded by hostile suburbs." And by spring 1977, Monsignor Baroni's ideas were enshrined, as it were, in the "National Neighborhood Policy Act"—an act that holds promises along with the danger that the promises get strangled by rules, guidelines, and bureaucratic ineptness. President Carter appointed Baroni to administer the act.

While the monsignor moved into the office of under secretary in the Department of Housing and Urban Affairs, growing numbers of "young professionals" moved into working-class parishes. They are not all of them rueful suburbanites surging into the city. One survey of new urban pioneers (a sample of 57, representing twice that number, who bought old houses in the Mount Pleasant neighborhood of Washington, D.C., and were interviewed by George Washington University planning students in the summer of 1976) found that fewer than one-fifth came from the suburbs.

One-third of them had children, but only half of the children attended public schools. All of them reported substantial incomes, yet almost all of them did rehabilitation work themselves. Along with exposed brick walls, butcher blocks, skylights, and hanging plants, that is part of the urban chic.

Despite often hostile receptions ("The first day we were here, a little kid came up and announced he was going to slash our tires."), burglaries, vandalism, hopelessly irregular trash collection, dirty streets, rats, noise, smells, and sore muscles from scraping endless layers of paint from Victorian mantels, 86 percent of the pioneers said they were happy to have moved to Mount Pleasant and would do it again.

28 Power to the People

To make neighborhoods work, neighborhood residents need control over neighborhood destinies. We must rehabilitate not only old houses, but the old neighborhood organizations. They existed in the days of Boss Tweed and Tammany Hall, but earlier in this century the political reformers threw them out, along with the old ward heelers. But, in a sense, the old precinct or ward "machines" represented "citizen participation" and "participatory democracy," although they were often corrupt.

"Real citizen participation is possible," wrote zoning lawyers Richard F. Babcock and Fred P. Bosselman, "only if real governmental power is delegated to the neighborhood level. It is past time that we begin directing imaginative debate toward the formulation of a legal and administrative system that may achieve real decentralization of governmental power in our large cities and still leave to the central city government control over those features of the urban environment that require centralized administration."

Elected neighborhood councils, commissions, or whatever, should be given legal authority to attain the neighborhood objectives, protect the neighborhood environment, expedite public services, and stimulate the neighborhood's cultural and social life.

This goes further than Babcock and Bosselman, who would

grant the neighborhood only the power to act as a zoning board. Their neighborhood board would set standards, enforce them, and grant variations from them. The standards and their enforcement would be subject, of course, to the overall policies and guidelines laid down by the city.

Unquestionably this presents the clear danger that some neighborhood government will be reactionary and exclusionary. Conflicts with regional planning and regional policy are unavoidable. But they can be resolved—if often by compromise—and a system of conflict resolution by elected representatives, rather than judges, must be devised as regional or metropolitan development corporations are established. We cannot place urban planning and environmental decisions at the mercy of the courts. They are not equipped to adjudicate them and they don't want to adjudicate them any more than they want to decide whether or not a hernia operation is indicated. City planning by court order is usually bad city planning.

Variations in the size of neighborhoods should not present a political problem. The states of our union also vary in population. The people in the neighborhood can still be equally represented on the city council, as the citizens of the states are equally represented in the House of Representatives.

Nor do I see any reason why all neighborhood councils in a city need to start at the same time. All neighborhoods must be equally empowered, but it should be up to the citizens whether and when they wish to exercise this power. In other words, if some neighborhoods are eager to go, and others are dallying and quarreling, there is no reason the eager ones should not be allowed to proceed.

Proceed with what?

Finding and affirming their identity, in the first place. In the case of historic neighborhoods, this will be quite simple. Everyone can see that the old houses, the brick pavement, and the old trees are distinct and special.

Other neighborhoods have unique natural or man-made features. They are located on a hill, or along a river or lake front. They are the hinterland of a prominent city square or other landmark.

The neighborhood council has the task of recognizing and strengthening the specific character of the neighborhood. In some instances, a landmark or symbol may have to be created. Cincinnati, having launched a "nuclear neighborhood program," has, for instance, chosen an old market hall, Findlay Market, as well as the Cincinnati Music Hall, as the focal points of two nuclei.

In the look-alike suburbs, the landmark might be a shopping center, a church, or, if all else fails, a lookout tower built just for the pleasure of it.

That landmark or symbol is vital. You have to be able to see what you belong to. The next step is to give it emphasis. Cincinnati renovated Findlay Market, put it back into operation, and then proceeded to build a center for social services across the street. The center, a brightly painted, remodeled building complex, includes educational aid, employment services, a credit union, a welfare office, a post office, and a library, all in one building. A second building serves senior citizens. A third building is devoted to parent-child activities and counseling. And a fourth building houses recreation activities, including a skating rink and an indoor swimming pool. The four buildings enclose a landscaped court.

Every neighborhood will want to have a center of this kind— some more and some less ambitious. Plans for it, including the financing, would be worked out in public meetings and committee sessions.

Ideally, the public services of a neighborhood are clustered in one place, as in Cincinnati, and as in medieval European towns, where all these civic institutions were located on the market square in front of the cathedral. But there are other ways to give form and prominence to the neighborhood's municipal functions. There is the linear arrangement in the American Main Street tradition, for instance. The new services offer a great opportunity to put handsome old buildings to use. Good graphics—colorful directional signs and symbols—can do wonders.

It is equally important to mark the boundaries of the neighborhood clearly, because you can't feel at home in a place that doesn't have a beginning and an end. If there is no obvious boundary, such as a river, a freeway, a heavy traffic artery, or greenbelt, a narrow strip of grass, trees, and shrubbery will do—it is better to paint the sidewalk in bright orange than to have no visible boundary at all. Good neighborhoods make good fences.

The city's planners are likely to have ideas about how the neighborhood ought to develop, ideas for more commerce here, more low-income housing there, more or less density. The neighborhood council must have the right to accept, reject, or amend these plans.

In the end, I am convinced, we shall get more environmental protection, historic preservation, sensible public transportation, and racial and economic integration by way of open and frank political planning in which all parties and interests participate as equal partners, than by meaningless planning commission gobbledygook.

Beyond planning and zoning, the neighborhood councils should also have powers to improve the much talked about quality of life.

In the first, tenuous year of their existence, the Advisory Neighborhood Commissions in Washington, D.C.—making up for lack of any real clout with the unpaid devotion of elected commissioners—can boast of tangible accomplishments. The Southwest commission has improved urban renewal plans and security and fire protection in a public housing project. The Capitol Hill commission held hearings on meter reading and billing practices of the gas company and kept the city from discontinuing nighttime bus service. In Adams-Morgan, the commission brought English and Spanish-speaking people together to turn low-income renters into owners. The Dupont Circle ANC stopped the highway department from turning off street lights, arguing that crime is more expensive than electricity.

Neighborhood citizen councils should be able to compel proper building maintenance, to enforce architectural standards, and to make the city clean its streets, maintain its parks, and enforce its sanitation rules.

Some neighborhoods are a bit finicky and humorless about imposing codes. It can be exasperating to be told how often to cut the lawn, what color to paint the shutters, or what kind of trees to plant in the front yard.

But let's not get rigid about other people's rigidity. At this period of urban messiness and decay, I would rather err on the side of zealous order. Conformity has never struck me as quite the evil the conformist, liberal cliché has made it out to be. Most people want to conform.

A person who feels very strongly about expressing his individuality by way of tall grass, purple shutters, and fruit trees

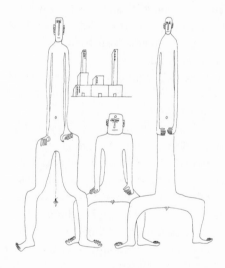

that attract wasps should not buy a house in a finicky neighborhood.

In most cities that have architectural review boards, visual harmony was advanced without stifling diversity and originality. The government protects us from poisoned food. I see no reason why society should not protect itself from ugliness.

Tastes change, of course. So should fine arts commissions and architectural controls. It is simple. The commissioners and controllers should be appointed only once and for limited, staggered terms. They should also consist predominantly of citizen representatives rather than architects and planners. Architects like to think that only architects should be allowed to discuss and judge architecture, which is like saying that only pig farmers should be allowed to eat pork.

29 Block Kiosk

In the suburbs and in the city, neighborhoods consist of blocks. And each block, I propose, should have its block kiosk, or block pavilion, or, if these words are too fancy for you, call it block house.

The block kiosk, as I see it, is a place somewhere between the family living room and the neighborhood center, a place where, on a nice day, people are likely to come in their bathrobes and slippers.

Block kiosks should be simple structures that provide shelter, include a locker for every family living on the block, benches and picnic tables, soft drink and coffee vending machines to whet spontaneous coffee klatsches, and maybe a laundromat and other conveniences.

Much like the old small town general store, the kiosks would serve as home distribution and service centers. We badly need them, or something like them. Home delivery of groceries, milk, fresh bread, and other goods is already a half-forgotten legend. Mail and even newspaper delivery is in trouble due to rising wages and transportation costs.

Pick-up of trash and garbage is also in trouble. It is one of our most difficult urban problems. Garbage men strike with increasing frequency. And every time there is a strike, there is a severe health hazard, to say nothing of the stench.

We shall, before long, have to establish distribution centers in both cities and suburbs that reduce the number of stops for deliveries and pick-ups and are still within convenient walking distance for people. They exist, in a sense, in high-rise buildings, where people pick up their mail and deliveries in the lobby, and where trash and garbage is either picked up or disposed of in one place.

The logical place, the lobby of horizontally arranged dwellings, is the block kiosk.

In the city, the kiosk might be placed at every other intersection, so each would serve four blocks. In the suburbs, it might be placed in cul-de-sacs. The location in either case might lead to a rerouting of traffic that would make the closing, or partial closing of streets possible so they can be used as parks and playgrounds.

Block kiosks need not be new buildings. In Copenhagen, an old trolley barn was turned into an adventure playground. In Washington, an old telephone equipment warehouse rotting in an alley was converted into a neighborhood center. There are many unused spaces in the city that could be "recycled" for this purpose.

But if our entire urban distribution system is to be reorganized, we shall need so many block kiosks that their basic components might have to be prefabricated. That would not frighten me, because in the hands of good designers, they could still provide variety and individuality, to harmonize with the buildings they serve and to give each area its own colorful identity. I hope they will sport flagpoles or tall posts, perhaps towers, to add exclamation marks to the prosaic monotony of most subdivisions.

People will go to the pavilion in the morning to pick up their mail. Some will do so on their way to work—for the kiosk can also be the pick-up point for the car pool or bus. Some people will stop awhile to linger and chat and park their children at the tot lot.

Neighbors will find fresh dairy products and packages delivered there. The place will have vending machines for cigarettes, shoelaces, aspirin, film, or whatever might suddenly be needed—thus saving a trip to the supermarket.

They will bring their trash as well as used bottles, newspapers, and other items for recycling.

There should be laundromats, not only for the laundry but to recreate the village well, where people gather and gossip. In La Clede Town, a downtown community in St. Louis, architect Chloethiel Woodard Smith designed a separate place for the public washing and drying machines, equipped them with coffee automats and a few tables and chairs, and warmed the neighborhood spirit by at least ten degrees.

All block pavilions should have mailboxes and postage stamp vending machines, installed by the postal service, to avoid the rip-off of our drugstore stamp machines.

There might be "fix-it-yourself-shops" where neighbors can

share tools and know-how for home repairs and remodeling. They might include a "tinker library." It is a place where people take broken appliances like radios, toasters, clocks, and record players. Mechanically inclined youngsters come and take them apart, use the parts for the repair of similar gadgets, build new ones, and tinker around.

For real convenience, the block kiosk should be open around the clock, or at least until late in the evening. There should be a human being, a tyrant or saint, neighborhood godfather or mother confessor. The attendant would have roughly the functions of the concierge in French apartment houses.

Concierges feel fiercely possessive about their domains and everyone in them. They watch, guard, baby-sit, keep the key for your aunt if she arrives before you do, challenge suspicious-looking strangers, water the flowers, mow the lawn and otherwise keep the place tidy, know all the gossip, protect everyone's morals, and are, in countless other ways, the pepper in the urban stew.

This might be a desirable job for students or retired folks, an interesting job that would leave some time for studying and other pursuits. Like the buildings and their upkeep, it should probably be paid for in part out of real estate taxes and in part out of state taxes. Kiosks would be a public utility that enhances the environment and helps save energy.

I have only one caveat about them. In my block at least, Muzak or loud radios should be strictly prohibited. The block pavilion should not be an irritant, but a way to enhance livability.

Livability is enhanced in many ways—the arrangement and rearrangement of buildings and open space, or planting more trees and greenery. Trees reduce heating and cooling costs. In summer, tree shade reduces the temperature. They break winter chill and baffle wind tunnel effects caused by other buildings. They muffle noise. They cleanse the air of dust and other pollutants. Any builder, traffic engineer, or other vandal who chops down a living city tree must be forced to replant it.

We should add more color to the cityscape by decorating

streets and public places with sculpture and murals, by open-air concerts, performances, dancing on the streets, festivals and ceremony.

We are new at settling down to enjoy public life. Some neighborhoods may need help. They will want to draw on the expertise of the city planning department. They may be sufficiently served by volunteer talent in their own midst. They may wish to hire consultants.

A French innovation of the 1950s is worth considering. To strengthen the means of social cohesion in the new, satellite communities it is building around Paris and other big cities, the French government has formed teams of *"animateurs."* The task of the team is to animate and stimulate the social and cultural life in the new communities, assist people to get settled, act as ombudsmen, and provide liaison with builders, schools, and public authorities. Each team consists of representatives of different government departments and experts in adult education, sports, youth guidance, and public health. The different government agencies pay the salaries of their representatives.

The job of these urban animators is not to impose or prescribe social relations or advance ready-made solutions, but to explore new ways for the community to act as a community.

In New York City, the animator was the fiscal crisis. As Neal R. Peirce reported in his syndicated column on urban affairs, the crisis started "a sense of small-town community spirit and cooperation, sprouting on the city's blocks." It is helped along by a "New York Self-Help Handbook," published by the Citizens Committee for New York City.

As Peirce tells it, the handbook starts with a section on community crime prevention, including block-watcher programs, civilian car and foot patrols, and auxiliary police officer and alarm systems. It goes on to parent safety patrols, property identification systems, and a buddy alarm system for merchants.

Fire prevention comes next and there are programs for block cleanups, sidewalk sweeps, litter baskets, graffiti removal, recycling centers, neighborhood dog runs, and antilitter campaigns. There are also programs in community gardening, playlots, mural painting, bench painting, and how citizens can adopt and care for street trees.

The handbook reviews many programs for children, ranging from street olympics and volunteer tutorial programs, to trips for youth, family day care, and turning residential blocks into daytime play streets. For senior citizens, there are suggestions for local merchant discount programs, medical and food supply delivery to homebound people, escort services, and telephone reassurance.

Of New York City's 35,000 blocks, reports Peirce, some 10,000 have organized block associations. Many of these have begun to replace New York's declining political clubs as mini-governments on the grassroots level.

Jackie and Dennis Canning are singled out in the column, because they organized their Brooklyn block to drive out prostitutes and drug pushers. One of their methods: bombarding pimps with balloons filled with water from rooftops. (Friends of mine who live on Washington's Logan Circle use a less strenuous method. They conspicuously take down the license numbers of the "johns.")

New York's effort shows that neighborhood self-help need not be turned into another costly bureaucratic program. It should be a voluntary effort, paid for by citizen self-assessment for specific projects, by foundations and businesses. What better advertising than a modest little plaque that tells you that this park bench, or fountain, or playground, or block kiosk was donated by the friendly folks who bring you Schlock beer.

The block kiosk, while serving a vital function as a distribution point, could be a new catalyst for citizen action on behalf of a more civilized life.

30 Recycling Cities

Urban renewal, thank heaven, has been replaced by urban rehabilitation. The bulldozer has been replaced by hammer, trowel, and paintbrush. The government's urban renewal program concentrated on the central business district. The spontaneous citizen rehabilitation effort began in the neighborhoods.

At first, the newspaper real estate sections asserted that urban reclamation confined itself to "trendy" places, like Boston's Back Bay and South End, Philadelphia's Society Hill, Baltimore's Charles Village, Washington's Capitol Hill and North Dupont Circle, and San Francisco's Noe Valley.

But white, middle-class, old-house enthusiasts, armed with paint remover and putty knives, have been spotted in Norfolk, Virginia; Paterson and Wilmington, New Jersey; Cincinnati and Dayton, Ohio; St. Louis, Missouri; Santa Fe, New Mexico; Galveston, Texas . . .

"Pioneers, trend-setters, are followed by colonists, by consumers who have been educated through the example of others about what is desirable. If a settlement 'takes,' it will invariably be because of the presence of 'followers' who make up the bulk of demand for any commodity or fashion, whether it happens to be Victorian mini-mansions or flared trousers or whatever else. However, these trends in living choices do not advertise themselves until a later stage. The critical period has typically occurred when planners and policy makers [or real estate editors] were hardly watching, or unaware of what to watch for," says a study on the evolution of city neighborhoods, by the Parkman Center for Urban Affairs in Boston.

The middle-class "colonization" of the lower-class city has turned the corner in Philadelphia, at this writing the only city in America where more white middle-class people are moving in than are moving out. Invaders have conquered Baltimore's Fells Point. Having firmly established themselves on Washington's Capitol Hill, they are now moving in on Logan Circle. From Boston, Massachusetts, to Louisville, Kentucky, and St. Paul, Minnesota, inner-city rehabilitation is making enormous strides in virtually all old American cities.

The new frontier, like the old one out West, seems remarkably similar wherever you go. In Philadelphia's Washington Square West, I recently found messy streets, neat and tree shaded streets, narrow cobblestone alleys and passageways, old warehouses, churches, fire houses, deserted houses, restored houses, flamboyantly rebuilt houses, surprises, squalor, and elegance.

Neatly dressed children bicycle and tricycle on neatly dressed, narrow streets around old horse troughs and among pots of geraniums. A stout woman leans over the balcony railing and noisily cusses out the man who is sweeping the gutter. For lack of a garage, the garage sale on Lombard Street is held on the sidewalk. Everyone here seems straight out of suburbia. Old-timers don't hold garage sales. They sit on their stoops and chat, or they take chairs and bridge tables out on the sidewalk and play cards in the sun.

What with the Jewish textile stores on Fourth Street, the boutiques and antique stores along South Street, the Camac Market, the prim streets around the Kosciusko Polish Club in Queen Village, there is more variety here on an hour's walk than on many a day's drive through suburbia.

The new pioneers want to keep it that way.

The young architects, lawyers, writers and such who are turning old house shells into a new way of life are enthusiastic and optimistic. They talk of the wonder of being able to walk not only to work but also to four legitimate theaters, a dozen major movies, four department stores, many shops, and some good restaurants.

The new families have organized a baby-sitter cooperative, and persuaded the city to revise plans for Seeger Park to include more playgrounds for children.

But for all the talk, there seems to be little, if any, personal contact, let alone integration, of rich and poor, black and white, ethnic and Wasp in Washington Square West. Nor is there much in other neighborhoods on the new urban frontier that are privately rehabilitated by the white middle class.

In Washington Square West, the poor blacks and a good many Poles are suspicious that the renovating newcomers will drive them out. The Polish church is losing members. The desire for a mixed neighborhood seems one-sided. It is intellectual idealism on the part of the newcomers, a form of inverted snobbism, perhaps. The Vassar graduate occasionally talks to the black or Polish woman on the street about the children or the garbage collection. There is, if we are honest about it, not enough conversation left over for house visits, let alone dinner.

So how do you keep a neighborhood mixed and integrated? How do you attract taxpaying, middle-income people back into the city without displacing and uprooting poor people? Every time someone moves in, someone else has to move out. If the movers-in are richer than the movers-out, real estate speculation sets in, accelerates the process, and can make it cruel for the poor.

There is no question that heterogeneity is desirable, and most pioneers, like my friends on Washington Square West, find it desirable.

They—and I—desire racially and economically mixed neighborhoods because we want pluralism and social, as well as political, democracy. You cannot have that without pluralistic and democratic settlements, that is, by providing equal access to the advantages and benefits a good living environment offers—from beautiful views and outdoor recreation, to good schools and good municipal services.

Everyone in America, particularly our minorities, knows from bitter experience that separate is never equal.

But as middle-class colonization progresses and property values rise, the second wave of invaders becomes more class-conscious and pushes for homogeneity. This is not a matter of race, but of class. The pioneering, young professionals have from the beginning included black professionals. Blacks feel no differently than their white colleagues about a family of next-door neighbors headed by a welfare mother with 12 children, no manners, and a front yard that resembles (and smells like) the town dump. It's "black and white, shoulder-to-shoulder against the lower classes," as Mike Nichols quipped in the late fifties, when the integrated faculty of the University of Chicago opposed a public housing project in adjacent Hyde Park Kenwood.

Neighborhood integration must nevertheless be pursued. A condition is that all neighbors—colonizers and colonials—agree to integrate, improve the neighborhood, rehabilitate the houses, keep the streets and public spaces clean and green.

This requires that the poor be helped. It requires low-interest rehabilitation loans for them. It requires that renters be turned into owners.

Various cities have various programs to achieve this, most public, some private. Pittsburgh pioneered government-guaranteed, low-cost rehabilitation loans to help old residents keep up with the newly arrived Joneses. In Washington, D.C., citizens of the Adams-Morgan neighborhood blocked construction of a Perpetual Federal Savings and Loan Association branch office, until the bank agreed to provide loans for as much as 90 percent of the purchase price for moderately priced homes and for nonprofit housing cooperatives, as well as other services to the residents. For the federal government, rehabilitation loan guarantees for the old residents of recovering neighborhoods are probably the least expensive and safest way to provide desperately needed low-income housing.

Security for such loans is the city's effort to do its share for recovery by sprucing up streets and sidewalks, parks and playgrounds, and introducing imaginative improvements, such as an agreeable traffic pattern and some green spots. Most of all, the cities must set up adequate service and maintenance programs.

In short, while a variety of public and private programs are required to make the city what it ought to be, urban rehabilitation is proving itself far more efficient than the other urban improvement programs we have tried.

As Bruce K. Chapman, a member of the President's Advisory Council on Historic Preservation, has recently pointed out, "preservation is as much as 30 percent cheaper now than new construction. It takes less time. It saves energy and natural resources. It retards urban sprawl. It also generates more jobs: According to statistics from the Department of Commerce, one million dollars on preservation creates an average of 109 jobs, compared with an average of 69 jobs for new construction."

That is important.

It is, as I said earlier, nonsense to pretend that we can provide employment for Harlem's or Bedford-Stuyvesant's un-employed by luring manufacturing industries back into these places. The industries, at the very least, would want their trucks to move. So the city gives them a freeway for $200 million a mile and displaces thousands of people and small businesses in order to employ—how many? A modern, automated plant employs, say, 100 engineering school graduates in white smocks, who grudgingly commute from Shady Orchards or Sunny Meadow out in Tomahawk County, plus six janitors and four cleaning women who live and pay taxes in the inner city.

This is not to say that there should not be any efforts to create more blue-collar employment in the city center. But it must be the right kind of employment.

Robert S. McNamara and his World Bank learned this in developing countries. The World Bank would proudly invest millions in a shining new shoe factory, expecting to put the whole country on its feet. Instead, more people were barefoot than ever because the factory used efficient plastic and rubber materials, employed an efficient maximum of 40 employees, and efficiently deprived 500 tanners, 5,000 shoemakers, and 12,000 goat herders of their livelihood.

Ghetto youngsters have little hope of finding jobs in what McNamara calls "the formal sector" of the economy—the large corporations. There is greater hope for them in "the informal sector"—small businesses and what economists call "labor intensive" enterprises.

Small stores, specialty shops, little Greek or Mexican restaurants, markets and pushcarts with fresh, uncellophaned fruits and vegetables, pizzas or quiches, freshly baked breads and cakes, shoeshine parlors, custom tailors, book binderies, secondhand book stores, repair shops for silverware, musical instruments, and furniture are the salt of city civilization. We can use a big dose of that salt to make the plastic-encased, ready-made junk more palatable. There is creative and meaningful work for enterprising spirits, aside from scented-candle boutiques.

"It is not that we don't need every person in this country," Margaret Mead told a congressional committee. "It is that we have a system where we can't use them . . . We haven't enough people to take care of children. We haven't enough people to take care of the aged or to keep the park clean or to deal with pollution. If we looked at what we need in this country, we need every human being and we could use every single human being we have got."

But rather than inspire initiative and pride in handiwork, being of service to others, and the learning of skills, authorities usually harass and discourage small business enterprise and competition with silly regulations, stiff license fees, and other red tape.

The largest stepping-stone out of the ghetto is urban reclamation. With one act of Congress, or, for that matter, a state legislature or city council, we could provide job training, jobs, and housing. The act would recruit young men and women in the inner city to wield hammers, paintbrushes,

shovels, and rakes, rather than switchblades and spray cans. They could rehabilitate deteriorated houses and apartments, "recycle" abandoned buildings to productive use—community workshops, day-care centers, health clinics, and meeting places for the elderly. They could clean and maintain public spaces.

Such Urban Reclamation Brigades (as we might call them to get the acronym URBs) would resemble Franklin Roosevelt's Civilian Conservation Corps that employed thousands during the depression. President Carter talked about reviving the idea in his election campaign. It should be taken seriously.

A good many new jobs can be created rehabilitating the slums to provide more and better low-income housing.

But we must also be realistic about the poor. Houses cannot be rehabilitated without money, which must be paid with higher rents or mortgage payments. Before the public pays to rehabilitate the homes and neighborhoods of the poor, the public must be sure that continued residence offers them opportunities for escaping poverty. If it does not, why saddle them with another hopeless burden? In the first five years of the Bedford-Stuyvesant rehabilitation program launched by

Robert Kennedy, public loans of $18 million spruced up 120 buildings with anywhere from two to 47 apartments each. Bedford-Stuyvesant is no better off. There are still at least 14,000 abandoned buildings.

What that says is not that we should despair on slum rehabilitation. We need more of it. But it is not a sufficient long-range answer. Rehabilitation of the slums will never by itself create all the blue-collar jobs needed in the city. It does not improve job qualifications for youngsters who were never properly taught, or reduce commuting costs to the new employment opportunities outside the center city.

Slum rehabilitation therefore cannot be allowed to weaken, let alone substitute for, an energetic national effort to bring people and jobs together in planned and integrated satellite communities.

In other words, we should not worry that poor people may be forced to move out of miserable slums that they cannot themselves rebuild. We should worry about where they are moving and the life they can build there for themselves.

31 The New Architecture

Judith Martin, the writer, recently needed an architect. Or, rather, she found herself on a committee appointed to select an architect who would design a simple theater/gymnasium for the school her children attend. She sent for the American Institute of Architects' booklet, "You and Your Architect," dedicated to "those contemplating a construction project." She followed the rules listed under "How Do I Find the Right Architect?"

She and her committee scheduled appointments with six distinguished architects who said they were interested in the project. But the first one never showed up for his appointment, and the second repeatedly stressed how much he and his team enjoyed doing "fun buildings." About that reportedly leaky roof on one of his buildings, he said it was probably the fault of the roofer or some other construction team. True, his firm had "supervised" the building, but "supervising is not superintending, you understand."

The next architect was for fun through color. He said his firm had studies to prove that teenagers preferred primary colors to somber colors. Another prospect recommended "vibrancy" and "drama" through the use of skylights. "Actually," mused Martin, "we had hoped to achieve vibrancy and drama more cheaply by filling the place with kids."

Then there was the team that showed up with slides of yachts bobbing in the water, a lone guitar propped against an empty conversation pit, skiers climbing a mountain, and Man Walking on the Moon, the last being a slide available from the gift shop of the Smithsonian's Air and Space Museum. The show took two slide machines and a separate sound machine to supply recorded guitar accompaniment. "At first," said Martin, "I thought they were showing us their work, and felt that anybody who could do that snow-covered mountain could do my school's annex any day. But it turned out that this was only 'to show where we're all coming from' and I was told, 'don't worry about it.' "

So she and her committee did not worry and picked the sixth architect, who warned them that the building might look like a box, but talked about versatile, durable flooring.

"I felt badly that in my speech nominating him," she said, "I stressed the fact that he hadn't promised us anything original or dramatic or vibrant. I meant it as a compliment."

It should be taken as one.

If architecture, as Mies van der Rohe said, "is the translation

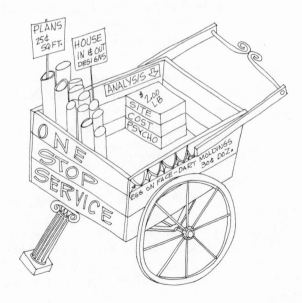

of the will of an epoch into space," only the sixth architect translated the spirit correctly.

The other contenders for that $350,000 theater/gymnasium may have been right that, a while ago, the will of the epoch wanted "fun buildings," "vibrancy," "drama," and "where it's at." But now the will has changed, or is, at any rate, changing. We see that the blessings of technology are being offset by its curses. And it is no longer our will, as John Gardner put it, to "sit like a Croesus on a garbage heap." If we want a theater that will also serve as a gymnasium for the kids, we want a theater that will also serve as a gymnasium for the kids.

It is no longer our will to build buildings which, with their needless heating and air-conditioning, wasteful use of materials, excessive illumination, automatic controls, and all the rest, consume "twice the electricity that was used 25 years ago for all purposes," according to architect Richard G. Stein. New buildings, Stein says in his carefully researched book, *Energy and Architecture,* consume well over one-third of all the energy used in the United States. Add to that the waste of urban sprawl.

For this reason alone, to say nothing of the psychological dissatisfaction with "fun buildings," we need to go back to the drawing board. We need a new urban vision. We need a new architecture.

The first thing to be said is that a new architecture does not mean revival of some old architectural style. Nostalgia is no guide to the future, which is where we will spend the rest of our lives. We need historic continuity. We need to learn from the accumulated experience of the past. We don't need phony Howard Johnson Colonial any more than we need to wear powdered wigs.

The second caveat in the search for a new architecture is just that. As Gropius once said, "We need more search and less research." Architecture, urbanism, art, and human behavior cannot be reduced to statistics. Nor can anything make them a science. To pretend that they are by misapplying scientific methodology or inventing jargon is not science but charlatanry (or cheap salesmanship). It is, as sociologist James Coleman of the University of Chicago has said, "a little unfortunate that social science has come to occupy as central a position as it has today." We must learn to trust common sense.

This includes common sense about what architects call "energy efficient" building. There is a great danger of architects seeking magic formulas to solve our problems, as they did at the beginning of the modern revolution. The current abracadabra emanating from the public relations offices of the American Institute of Architects is that solar energy collectors will bring salvation. They won't. They are a nice gesture, says Richard G. Stein, like the wartime posters proclaiming "We Do Our Part."

The installation of solar collectors, with the necessary storage provisions and heat exchangers, on 25 percent of all homes and apartments in the United States, in ten years would cost $345 billion, Stein figures—if it were possible. Assuming the gadgets would supply 75 percent of the energy needs of the households that pay for them, it would save 3.3 percent of our present total energy requirements. These requirements keep growing at the rate of at least 1 percent a year. So in the end, we would not be better off.

In other words, catching a little sunshine won't do. It would be more helpful if architects learned where the sun rises and where it sets, and that there are climatic differences between Maine and Florida. We need to revive solar architecture.

Until the Abstract movement came along, practically everything built revolved, like the earth itself, around the sun. In palaces or huts, north, south, east, or west, the use of materials, the orientation of the building, the window and door openings, the roof structure, the height of rooms, and the shape of the building were determined by sun, wind, and rain.

Rational consideration of the climate, including the micro-climate—climatic variations of a specific location within a zone—will radically change our architecture. We will again see breezeways, awnings, roof overhangs, interior courts. We will see what Frank Lloyd Wright called "organic architecture"—buildings and communities designed *with* nature, not in defiance of nature.

Mies said "Less is more." I suggest architects do more with less. Our structures, as mentioned, contain more material than stability and safety require. Even the most trivial buildings are designed like massive fortresses, weighing down the earth with enormous quantities of reinforced concrete. Insecurity? A Pharaonic necrophilia?

The irony is that modern engineering has come up with cable and tension structures that combine strength with seemingly weightless grace. It seems more appealing.

It is time to replace contrived complexity with sensible simplicity.

That much maligned Victorian era came up with sensible simplicity, serving a multiplicity of functions at once. Stein recalls the cast-iron kitchen range, for instance. It was a versatile cooking machine, with varied heat, ranging from roasting temperatures in the oven to back-of-the-stove warming. It had coils for heating water. It served as a space heater that turned the kitchen into a family room.

Despite years of talk about the energy crisis, few, if any, thoughtful architectural innovations have been proposed. The architectural stars keep winning awards for their glass towers, and their press relations people write releases telling how energy-saving and human they are. If you really want energy-saving ideas, don't look in the architectural journals. Look for them in the *Whole Earth Catalog*.

There is one notable exception: The government of Iran submitted a "Habitat Bill of Rights" to the United Nations "Habitat" Conference on Human Settlements at Vancouver in June 1977.

The handsomely illustrated 180-page document was drafted by five internationally known architects at several meetings at Persepolis under the auspices of the Iranian Ministry of Housing and Urban Development: José Luis Sert, former chairman of the Harvard School of Design; Moshe Safdie, the Israeli-born, Canadian architect of "Habitat 67"; B. V. Doshe, one of India's most prominent architects; Georges Candilis of France; and Nader Ardalan of Iran. The group was assisted by William Doebele, head of the Harvard School of City Planning.

The unpaid work of these men—easily thousands of hours— is not acknowledged, however. The Iranian government decided that Moshe Safdie, who is Jewish, might be objectionable to Arabs in the United Nations. Therefore the names of all authors were withheld.

The statement attempts to define in architectural terms "those qualities which contribute to the well-being of man, his family, and the community in which he lives." It sets down basic principles for architecture and community design that are likely to foster privacy, identity, spiritual well-being and growth, sense of spaciousness, man's relationship to nature, a feeling of neighborliness and belonging, and a sense of security.

It challenges much of the urbanistic wisdom set down in *The Athens Charter*.

The Habitat Bill of Rights deplores the deterioration of the quality of life within our human habitat; the loss of individual, family, and community identity; the abuse of natural resources; the misuse of technology; and the disintegration of a wholesome interaction between humans and nature.

Text and illustrations show how developing nations can learn from the mistakes of the rich industrialized nations, and stress building on indigenous traditions in architectural design and settlement patterns.

The "right" to a good place to live, says the charter, includes private outdoor space, flexibility in the design of a house to allow for the growth in the size and income of a family, and clearly defined private territory. Radical demands, come to think of it. Enough to send people to the scaffolds.

Individual apartments in apartment houses should be clearly

recognizable from the outside, the Bill of Rights asserts. Housing projects should have attractive gateways. There should be a minimum of reliance on mechanical climate control. Clusters of family dwellings should be designed so that people can get to know one another and live close to the natural landscape. Automobiles and other machinery should be kept out of the personal sphere. Low-income communities should not be isolated from the rest of a community.

The document urges governmental intervention and guidance, to prevent urbanization from continuing "to raise havoc in both the industrialized and developing world." The Iranian document does not say so, but the United States, too, needs to guide helter-skelter development. We can no longer afford to ignore the congressional mandate for a national urban growth policy, contained in the 1970 Housing Act. It needs political support.

Only politics—the interplay between citizens and their government—can bring order into the human habitat. Livability is as much of a human right as liberty. It demands the same eternal—and informed—vigilance.

Architecture and urban design, as well as engineering that is essential to both, are not mere embellishments. Educators should not teach them as a minor adjunct to art history. Newspaper editors should not relegate them to an occasional piece on the arts page. Television producers and politicians should not ignore them.

Citizens should realize that good living conditions affect their welfare as much as good working conditions, demanding the same active interest. There is only one environment, and its quality, for man or beast, is determined as much by architects as by oil company executives, by city planners as by economic planners.

Architecture has become too important to be left to architects alone. They need the informed and creative support of their client—the public—reminding them that architecture is a social art.

The new architecture will emerge from a new popular

concern for the beauty and efficiency of our buildings, neighborhoods, towns, cities, and regions, a concern based on knowledge and perception.

As the wise and humane urbanist, Charles Abrams, has said, "The touch of a hundred hands can have the patina of humanity."

Selected Reading

I The New Mood

Babcock, Richard F. *The Zoning Game: Municipal Practices and Policies.* University of Wisconsin Press, Madison, 1966.

Burchard, John, and Bush-Brown, Albert. *The Architecture of America: A Social and Cultural History.* Little, Brown, Boston, 1961.

Jacobs, Jane. *The Death and Life of Great American Cities.* Vintage Books, New York, 1961.

Mumford, Lewis. *The Culture of Cities.* Harcourt, Brace & World, Inc., New York, 1938.

———.*The City in History.* Harcourt Brace Jovanovich, New York, 1961.

———.*The Highway and the City.* Harcourt Brace Jovanovich, New York, 1963.

Myers, Phyllis, and Binder, Gordon. *Neighborhood Conservation: Lessons from Three Cities.* The Conservation Foundation, Washington, D.C., 1977.

Owen, Wilfred. *Cities in the Motor Age.* Viking, New York, 1959.

Reps, John W. *The Making of Urban America.* Princeton University Press, Princeton, 1965.

Rifkind, Carole. *Main Street: The Face of Urban America.* Harper & Row, New York, 1977.

Schneider, Kenneth R. *Autokind vs. Mankind: An Analysis of Tyranny, A Proposal for Rebellion, A Plan for Reconstruction.* Norton, New York, 1971.

Scott, Mel. *American City Planning Since 1890.* University of California Press, Berkeley, 1969.

Steegman, John. *Victorian Taste: A Study of the Arts and Architecture from 1830 to 1970.* MIT Press, Cambridge, Ma., 1970.
Von Eckardt, Wolf. *The Challenge of Megalopolis.* Macmillan, New York, 1963.

II Abstract Architecture

Banham, Reyner. *Theory and Design in the First Machine Age.* Praeger, New York, 1960.
Bayer, Herbert, and Gropius, Walter (eds.). *Bauhaus: 1919-1928.* Bradford, Boston, 1959.
Benevolo, Leonardo. *History of Modern Architecture.* MIT Press, Cambridge, Ma., 1971.
Blake, Peter. *Form Follows Fiasco: Why Modern Architecture Hasn't Worked.* Little, Brown, Boston, 1977.
———. *The Master Builders: Le Corbusier, Mies van der Rohe, Frank Lloyd Wright.* Knopf, New York, 1960.
Boudon, Philippe. *Lived-in Architecture: Le Corbusier's Pessac Revisited.* MIT Press, Cambridge, Ma., 1972.
Doxiadis, Constantinos A. *The Great Urban Crimes We Permit by Law.* Lycabettus Press, Athens, 1973.
Giedion, Sigfried. *Space, Time and Architecture: The Growth of a New Tradition.* Harvard University Press, Cambridge, Ma., 1967.
Kopp, Anatole. *Town and Revolution: Soviet Architecture and City Planning 1917-1935.* Braziller, New York, 1970.
Le Corbusier. *The Athens Charter.* Grossman, New York, 1973.
———. *The City of Tomorrow and Its Planning.* MIT Press, Cambridge, Ma., 1971.
———. *Looking at City Planning.* Grossman, New York, 1971.
———. *Towards a New Architecture.* Praeger, New York, 1946.
Newman, Oscar. *Defensible Space: Crime Prevention through Urban Design.* Macmillan, New York, 1972.
Pevsner, Nikolaus. *Pioneers of Modern Design from William Morris to Walter Gropius.* Museum of Modern Art, New York, 1949.
Shvidkovsky, A.O. (ed.), *Building in the USSR 1917-1932.* Praeger, New York, 1971.
Starr, S. Frederick. *Melnikov: Solo Architect in a Mass Society.* Princeton University Press, Princeton, 1978.
Von Eckardt, Wolf. *A Place to Live: The Crisis of the Cities.* Delacorte, New York, 1967.
Watkin, David. *Morality and Architecture: The Development of a Theme in Architectural History and Theory from the Gothic Revival to the Modern Movement.* Clarendon Press, Oxford, 1977.

Wingler, Hans M. *The Bauhaus: Weimar, Dessau, Berlin, Chicago.* MIT Press. Cambridge, Ma., 1969.

III Search for Community

Apgar, Mahlon IV (ed.). *New Perspectives on Community Development.* McGraw Hill, London, 1976.

Ash, Maurice. *Regions of Tomorrow: Towards the Open City.* Schocken Books, New York, 1969.

Canty, Donald (ed.). *The New City.* Published by Urban America, Inc., for the National Committee on Urban Growth Policy. Praeger, New York, 1969.

Creese, Walter L. *The Search for Environment: The Garden City Before and After.* Yale University Press, New Haven, 1966.

Derthick, Martha. *New Towns-In Town: Why a Federal Program Failed.* The Urban Institute, Washington, D.C., 1972.

Eichler, Edward P., and Kaplan, Marshall. *The Community Builders.* University of California Press, Berkeley, 1967.

Evans, Hazel (ed.). *New Towns: The British Experience.* Wiley & Sons, New York, 1972.

Golany, Gideon (ed.). *Strategy for New Community Development in the United States.* (Community Development Series No. 9), Dowden, Hutchinson & Ross, Stroudsburg, Pa., 1975.

Heckscher, August. *Open Spaces: The Life of American Cities.* Harper & Row, New York, 1977.

Howard, Sir Ebenezer. *Garden Cities of Tomorrow.* MIT Press, Cambridge, Ma., 1965.

Kaplan, Samuel. *The Dream Deferred: People, Politics, and Planning Suburbia.* Seabury Press, New York, 1976.

Macfadyen, Dugald. *Sir Ebenezer Howard and the Town Planning Movement.* MIT Press, Cambridge, Ma., 1970.

Meyerson, Martin; Terrett, Barbara; and Wheaton, William L.C. *Housing, People, and Cities.* McGraw-Hill, New York, 1962.

Osborn, Frederic J., and Whittick, Arnold. *The New Towns: The Answer to Megalopolis.* MIT Press, Cambridge, Ma., 1969.

Perloff, Harvey S., and Sandberg, Neil C. (eds.). *New Towns: Why—And For Whom?* Praeger, New York, 1973.

Schaffer, Frank. *The New Town Story.* Paladin, London, 1972.

Senior, Derek (ed.). *The Regional City: An Anglo-American Discussion of Metropolitan Planning.* Aldine Publishing, Chicago, 1966.

Stein, Clarence S. *Towards New Towns in America.* MIT Press, Cambridge, Ma., 1966.

IV The New Urban Vision

Brambilla, Roberto, and Longo, Gianni. *For Pedestrians Only: Planning, Design, and Management of Traffic-free Zones.* Whitney Library of Design, New York, 1977.

Breines, Simon, and Dean, William J. *The Pedestrian Revolution: Streets Without Cars.* Vintage Books, New York, 1974.

Gruen, Victor. *Centers for the Urban Environment: Survival of the Cities.* Van Nostrand Reinhold Co., New York, 1973.

―――.*The Heart of Our Cities, The Urban Crisis: Diagnosis and Cure.* Simon and Schuster, New York, 1964.

Hamdami Foundation. *Habitat Bill of Rights.* Presented by Iran to Habitat, the United Nations Conference on Human Settlements, Vancouver, Canada and Tehran, Iran, 1976.

McHarg, Ian L. *Design With Nature.* Natural History Press, Garden City, 1969.

Moynihan, Daniel P. *Toward a National Urban Policy.* Basic Books, New York, 1970.

Owen, Wilfred. *The Accessible City.* Brookings, Washington, D.C., 1972.

Redstone, Louis G. *The New Downtowns: Rebuilding Business Districts.* McGraw-Hill, New York, 1976.

Ritter, Paul. *Planning for Man and Motor.* Pergamon Press, Oxford, 1964.

Stein, Richard G. *Architecture and Energy: Conserving Energy Through Rational Design.* Anchor Press, New York, 1977.

Tetlow, John, and Gross, Anthony. *Homes, Towns, and Traffic.* Praeger, New York, 1968.

Venturi, Robert. *Complexity and Contradiction in Architecture.* Museum of Modern Art, New York, 1966.

Weissbourd, Bernard. *Satellite Communities: Proposal for a New Housing Program.* Center for the Study of Democratic Institutions, Santa Barbara. Undated.

Weissbourd, Bernard, and Channick, Herbert. "An Urban Strategy." Reprint from *The Center Magazine,* vol. I, No. 6, Sept. 1968. Center for the Study of Democratic Institutions, Santa Barbara.

Workskett, Roy. *The Character of Towns: An Approach to Conservation.* The Architectural Press, London, 1969.

Index

Composed in Times Roman by New Republic Books, Washington, D.C.

Printed and bound by The Maple Press, York, Pennsylvania.

Designed by Wolf Von Eckardt.